THE MODERN

KITCHEN GARDEN

THE MODERN

KITCHEN
GARDEN

DESIGN • IDEAS • PRACTICAL TIPS

Written and photographed by

Janelle McCulloch

images
Publishing

When the world wearies and society fails to satisfy, there is always the garden.

MINNIE AUMONIE

Published in Australia in 2011 by
The Images Publishing Group Pty Ltd
ABN 89 059 734 431
6 Bastow Place, Mulgrave, Victoria 3170, Australia
Tel: +61 3 9561 5544 Fax: +61 3 9561 4860
books@imagespublishing.com
www.imagespublishing.com

Copyright © The Images Publishing Group Pty Ltd 2011
The Images Publishing Group Reference Number: 935

National Library of Australia Cataloguing-in-Publication entry:

Author: McCulloch, Janelle.
Title: The modern kitchen garden: design, ideas
               and practical tips
ISBN: 9781864704211 (hbk.)
Subjects: Gardens.
               Kitchen gardens.
Dewey Number: 635.9

Edited by Debbie Fry

Designed by The Graphic Image Studio Pty Ltd, Mulgrave, Australia
www.tgis.com.au

Pre-publishing services by United Graphic Pte Ltd, Singapore

Printed on 140 gsm GoldEast Matt Art paper by Everbest Printing Co.
Ltd., in Hong Kong/China

IMAGES has included on its website a page for special notices in relation
to this and our other publications. Please visit www.imagespublishing.com.

CONTENTS

Gardening Notes

INTRODUCTION

There is something incredibly restorative about being in a garden, particularly a kitchen garden. Flowers, of course, are famous for their fragrances, forms and inspirational displays (witness the perennial popularity of Monet's garden at Giverny, for example), but there is something wonderfully satisfying about plucking a vegetable from its bed, brushing the soil off its roots and thinking about how you will cook it in the evening meal. Flowers look beautiful but fruit and vegetables nourish the body and the soul. Even their names sound delightfully whimsical and evocative: *Monstera deliciosa, Listada de Gandia, Rosa Bianca*.

At this point I must confess that I am not a very good gardener – which is shameful, really, as I come from a family of talented gardeners – but I don't think you need to be a good gardener in order to adore gardens. Actually, I think it's entirely possible to worship gardens even when you know next-to-nothing about cultivating them.

I believe, in fact, that my status of 'virgin gardener' has been a help rather than a hindrance in writing this book. I do know a little – enough to converse on the subject – but I certainly don't know as much as an experienced gardener does. Being a journalist though, I tend to ask a hundred questions, and being a virgin gardener, I tend to ask the kind of questions that others perhaps feel too shy to, in case they look foolish. One thing that I have learned is to always ask questions, no matter how silly, because most gardeners *love* answering them. Consequently, I've been able to write a book that falls somewhere between the weighty reference guides for serious horticulturalists and the easy-to-read, how-to manuals for those just starting out. It is by no means a comprehensive guide to planting a kitchen garden: there are dozens of books that will show you how to propagate seeds, prune espalier fruit trees, plan your crop rotation or refine your compost heap. Rather, my publishers and I wanted to create a book that offered a behind-the-hedges glimpse into some of the world's best kitchen gardens. In doing so, we hope to offer inspiration to everyone who might be considering planting a kitchen garden of their own, as well as those who have already established their own Villandry-style parterre. We also wanted to discover what the notable and obviously knowledgeable gardeners featured in the following pages have learned from their lives in the garden – because, as all gardeners know, inside information is something you can *never* have enough of.

So what inspired this book in the first place? Well, it was actually my grandparents, who once owned a magnificent kitchen garden by the sea in northern New South Wales, Australia. This wondrous garden, which was so beautiful that tourist buses used to stop there, formed an integral part of their gloriously undulating tropical farm. It was such a magical and captivating place for a child that some of my best childhood memories are rooted in this fertile soil. My grandparents grew all sorts of fruit and vegetables – bananas, pineapples, paw paws, beans, cabbages, carrots, leeks, lettuce, peas, potatoes, rhubarb, zucchini, sweet corn, spring onions – but the vegetable they were really passionate about was the tomato. They were so mad about this ruddy-cheeked little plant that they turned over much of their land to tomato crops, and subsequently became incredibly successful farmers. I think we must have had tomatoes for breakfast, lunch, afternoon tea,

dinner and dessert. Consequently, as an adult, I have come to loath them – even the scent of them sends me running.

Unfortunately, none of this valuable potager knowledge rubbed off on any of their grandchildren, and certainly not on me. I began working as a journalist, moved to London and became obsessed with fashion. The closest I came to anything garden-related for a long time was admiring Gucci's floral frocks.

Fast-forward 10 years, and how the earth turns. Not only is everyone else in fashion suddenly interested in all things botanic and madly pulling on their Chanel wellies to go out and plant a *petit potager,* but I, too, have started to remember the sheer Elysian joy of being in a garden. It may be a natural progression of my interest in architecture and design (in the last 10 years I have swapped writing about fashion for architecture), or it may simply be a matter of shifting interests – I'm older now, and no longer as concerned about hemlines and heel heights. Whatever the reason, I am grateful that I have rediscovered this dormant passion.

I am still a dreadful gardener, and I'm sure my grandmother would be quite ashamed as she looks down from her deckchair above, but I'm now a fully paid-up convert to the world of horticulture. I am also determined, like every other gardener, to improve my knowledge. In the last few months my partner and I have made the decision to leave the city and buy a big old country house in a pretty village called Olinda, in the hills east of Melbourne. The house is on half an acre, and while that's not a great deal of land, it will be enough to allow me to plant a little potager. Having visited some of the world's most beautiful kitchen gardens in the production of this book, I am full of inspiration.

Like many of my gardening friends, I have been seduced by the names and appearances of some of the more unusual and heirloom varieties of fruit and vegetables. The Royalty Purple Pod bean, for example, has become rather popular in certain gardening sets for its elegance and elongated beauty – it is the Elle Macpherson of vegetables. And Sweet Chocolate capsicum, is surely one of the most beautiful looking vegetables with its magnificent dark-chocolate colour. But perhaps the most talked vegetable about is the Purple Podded Dutch pea, a climbing pea that not only looks exquisite growing up a trellis or teepee but also tastes delicious, even uncooked. (On a side note, Thomas Jefferson's favourite vegetable was the pea, and he had a long-running contest with his farming neighbours about who would produce the first peas of the season.)

I have bought my first pair of gumboots – pink ones, from Joules in London – and have started planning our potager. I am hoping, with the kind of shy hope that one hides from one's partner in case they vehemently disagree, that we can eventually upgrade our tiny half-acre property to a full-blown country farm one day. (I am also hoping that by the time we do, tractors will have come out in automatic.)

Winston Churchill once said that we shape our buildings and then they shape us, and I think the same could be said of gardens. We try to create our gardens by giving them form, depth, dignity and character. But in the end, I think it's our gardens that give those things to us.

Janelle McCulloch

The time has come, the Walrus said,
to talk of many things
Of shoes and ships and sealing wax,
of cabbages and kings…
***THROUGH THE LOOKING GLASS*, LEWIS CARROLL**

CABBAGES AND KINGS:
A (Brief) History Of Kitchen Gardens And The Reinvention Of The Modern Potager

His Royal Highness Prince Charles has planted one at his London home Clarence House and has, of course, always had a walled version at his Highgrove Estate in the English countryside. First Lady of the United States Michelle Obama has taken the initiative and is digging up part of the White House lawn to make way for a presidential version, the first of its kind since Eleanor Roosevelt planted a Victory Garden during the Second World War. Leading Australian chef Stephanie Alexander has started a national movement to introduce them into primary schools. And everyone else – from famous chefs to creative gardeners and curious children alike – is making room for them in their country estates, community gardens and suburban backyards.

Over the last few years, the vegetable garden has had a magnificent renaissance as people have started to rediscover the delicious freshness of just-plucked produce and the sheer Elysian joy of living a slow-food-inspired, plot-to-plate life. As one media wit put it: 'The vegie patch has certainly come a long way – from its humble roots (pun intended) to the dinner tables – and dinner-table conversations – of British royals and US presidents'.

As a result of this growing interest worldwide, potagers such as those at Château de Villandry in the Loire Valley and the King's Garden at Versailles (*le potager du roi*) have seen increasing numbers of visitors as food and garden lovers alike flock to witness the horticultural elegance of these extraordinarily designed spaces. The kitchen garden movement has also produced a flow-on effect for farmers' markets, as discerning shoppers now take the time to ask questions about the produce they're buying in order to uncover the most delectable vegetables on offer. In today's increasingly health-focused world, vegetables have certainly become big business.

But kitchen gardens have always been around, even if they haven't been the focus of so much media attention. Many of the original kitchen gardens, which were known as a *jardin potager* in French, were small, geometric garden plots that were usually grown by monks or nuns and hidden behind the high stone walls of medieval monasteries. These gardens not only enabled the monks or nuns to be self sufficient, but were sanctuaries of meditation and prayer: they were places to retreat to, to reflect and remember God.

According to gardening writer Jennifer Bartlett, the term *jardin potager* first appeared in 1567, in the work *L'agriculture et maison rustique* by Charles Estienne and Jean Liébault. It's not surprising that the French were among the first to realise the benefits of a vegetable garden. They have always understood the connection between food and life, between gardens and nourishment, and between the spirit, the mind and the body.

In a note on terminology, a potager is usually quite formal in design and can also be ornamental, while a kitchen garden, which is English or American, is typically an informal vegetable garden. However, the terms are becoming more and more entwined as gardens everywhere take on characteristics of both the French and English styles.

One of the differences between French and English kitchen gardens is that the French have elevated edible gardens, like almost everything else they do, into art. They've taken the task of growing

food and made it aesthetically pleasing, choosing plants for their colour and form as much as their flavour and functionality, planting them in strikingly repetitive geometric patterns for full visual effect. It's a classic example of how beauty is as important as utility to the French. As a consequence, most French potagers are so well designed that being in them is like being in a painting.

Centuries after the first monastic potagers attracted the attention of passing travellers, potagers and kitchen gardens are again becoming popular. With today's renewed interest in health and wellbeing – and the increasing recognition that this wellbeing largely comes from what we eat – kitchen gardens are taking on more and more importance in the modern home.

One of the main differences between today's kitchen gardens and those of yesteryear is that we are usually challenged for space in our compact modern homes, and many of us are endeavouring to integrate gardens into our already tightly squeezed properties. This inadvertently brings our gardening style back to a similarity with the gardens of old, as we merge our flower and vegetable gardens, just as the monks used to do – though our reasons for doing so are different from those of the monks.

For many of us, our kitchen gardens have become havens, spiritual sanctuaries into which we escape from the world outside. It seems the monks had the right idea, after all.

GARDENS OF PLEASURE, PEACE AND PRODUCE

A HAND-PICKED SELECTION OF THE WORLD'S BEST POTAGERS

HEIDE

The garden is a love song, a duet between a human being and Mother Nature.

JEFF COX

THE ARTIST'S GARDEN

Much has been written about John and Sunday Reed and their home at Heide (now the site of the Heide Museum of Modern Art) over the years, and for good reason. It is one of the most intriguing stories in Australian history. It's also a complicated story; a romantic dream edged with tragedy, achievements, artists and love triangles, and far too complex to cover here. However, I'll try to outline the main dramatic narrative, because it's important to know the story in order to understand the gardens.

John and Sunday Reed were two of Australia's most influential art patrons. Their Bloomsbury-style life at the pastoral retreat known as 'Heide' (short for Heidelberg), on the banks of the Yarra River north of Melbourne, was a truly Arcadian idyll. Some of Australia's most talented artists gravitated to Heide, seeking inspiration, conversation, camaraderie, a calm place to work and perhaps also a little financial backing. The Reeds, who both came from wealthy families, encouraged these artists by creating a pastoral sanctuary out of an old dairy farm. They created a French provincial-style cottage from the former farm house, installed an impressive library filled with books, art magazines and journals, established a culture of idealism and eclecticism, and invited like-minded individuals to stay. (Although the guest list also depended on how the Reeds felt about the artists, and whether they fancied inviting them.) The artists who came, camped out and stayed included Albert Tucker, Sidney Nolan, John Perceval, Charles Blackman and Joy Hester. All were inspired by the Heide life, so reminiscent of France and the artists' colonies there. (There were also artist colonies emerging near Heide at the same time, at Montsalvat and other areas along the Yarra.) Sidney Nolan was so inspired – both by Heide and by Sunday Reed, who became his lover and his muse – that he painted 26 of his original 27 Ned Kelly works in the dining room of the tiny farmhouse. Theirs was a life full of dreams, hopes, ambitions and artistic accomplishments. Heide was their home. And the Reeds – the dynamic, inspirational, progressive, intellectual, richly layered Reeds – were their creative supporters.

There's far more to the story, of course – affairs, falling outs, disagreements, divorce and tragic deaths – and much of this drama is detailed in the many books about the lives of the Reeds and those who lived with them. But in this chapter, it is the garden that takes centre stage. Sunday's gardens, which included her beloved kitchen garden and the legendary Heart Garden (a memorial to her relationship with Nolan) make up the gentle centre of Heide. The gardens are where Sunday loved to spend most of her time, and it is the gardens that fed her visitors, filled her kitchen and nourished her soul.

Everyone who stayed at Heide was expected to work in the gardens or on the property. The Reeds were firm believers in the power of collaboration, but more importantly, Heide was a self-sustaining place, which Sunday Reed firmly advocated. The heiress wanted to lead a simple, holistic lifestyle and the kitchen garden was a large part of that, providing most of their vegetables from season to season. There was also an orchard for fresh fruit, a dairy for butter, milk and cream, and a chook shed for the eggs. For much of the time the Reeds were living at Heide, Australia was experiencing great deprivation due to the

war, so Heide's larder offered the kind of culinary riches that were rarely seen elsewhere. No wonder their visitors loved it.

But there were other reasons for planting the gardens at Heide. Sunday and John wanted to grow unusual and rare plants, and to establish a European ornamental garden, something Sunday had seen while spending time in Europe. Their plans were ambitious so they hired Neil Douglas, a gardener who was also an artist, to assist in designing and implementing the strategy of the garden. Douglas had already established a garden of note at his own house at Bayswater that was inspired by Monet's garden at

Giverny. The Reeds learned of his horticultural talents and, after visiting his house, asked him to stay at Heide to design what is now known as The Wild Garden on the south side of the house.

The first kitchen garden at Heide (there were three planted in the time that John and Sunday lived there; one in 1934, the second in 1967, and the third in 1979) was positioned near the farmhouse. With her famous energy and impatience, Sunday dug the first plot before the Reeds had even moved into the house. Neil Douglas later helped with the development and expansion of the plots. Sunday, with her usual pragmatism, had decided that she wanted a functional kitchen garden that was easy to be in, however she also wanted a wide variety of vegetables and herbs to use in her cooking. Sunday was also converting to vegetarianism, so took a deep interest in the kinds of varieties they were about to plant. In the end, Heide's kitchen garden included broad beans, peas, leeks, potatoes, marrows, silverbeet, strawberries, salsify and all manner of herbs.

The Reeds travelled to Europe in 1948 to spend a year in France, and when they returned they bought dozens of packets of seeds not readily available in Australia. These included sea kale, aubergine, asparagus, fennel and endive, all of which were grown and used in cooking at Heide.

The Reed's search for unusual seeds and vegetable varieties continued through the time they lived at Heide. Self-confessed plant collectors, they loved instructing friends to pick up new or rare seeds when they journeyed overseas. A 1969 list of herbs in the Heide archive features such varieties as mandrake, Good King Henry, costmary, woodruff and wild indigo.

Today, the kitchen gardens at Heide are still going strong. As part of a 2005–6 Museum Redevelopment Program the original kitchen garden was restored to its former glory, and once again serves up an impressive crop each season.

Produce from the Heide Kitchen Garden is used in the new café at Heide, Café Vue, supervised by leading Melbourne chef Shannon Bennett. Heide is open to the public every day except Monday. For details, visit www.heide.com.au or email info@heide.com.au

SUNLIGHT AND DESIGN

When designing your kitchen garden, one of the most important elements to consider is the sun. Some people forget that vegetables need lots of light to grow and position their gardens in the shade. Full sun is best for vegetable growth, although half a day of sun is usually enough to encourage development as well. If you're in the northern hemisphere, try to plant your garden in rows from the north to the south, with taller plants at the northern end. (Reverse this in the southern hemisphere so that taller plants are at the southern end.) This will ensure that all rows receive an equal amount of sunlight.

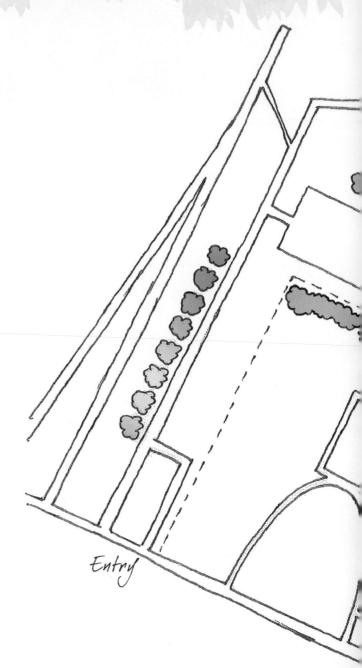

Entry

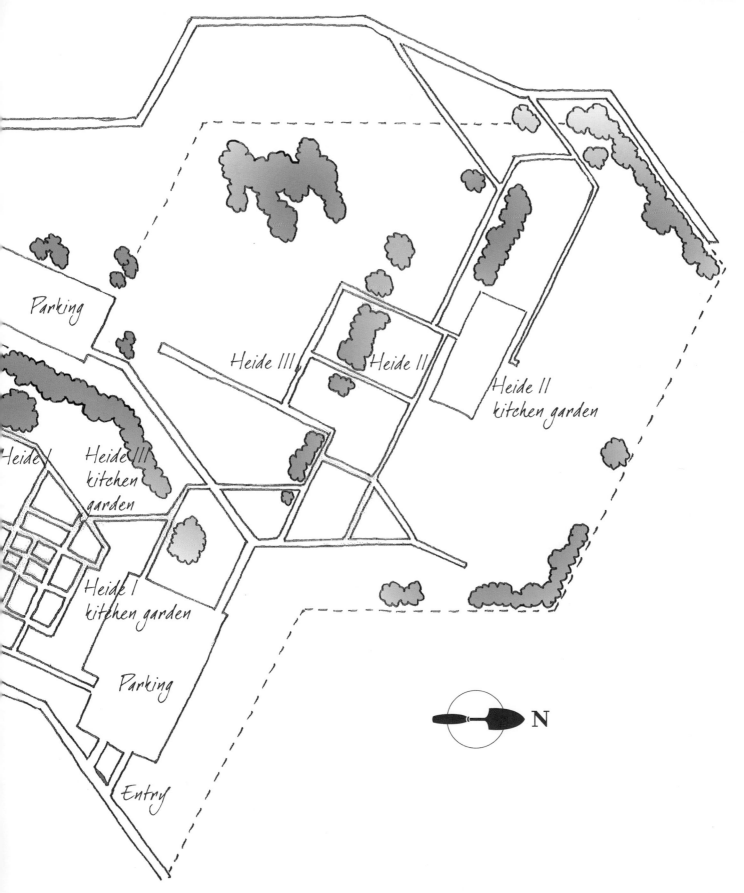

THE BOHEMIAN GARDEN

PETERSHAM HOUSE AND NURSERIES

A garden must combine the poetic and the mysterious with a feeling of serenity and joy.
LUIS BARRAGAN

There is nothing more enchanting than a walled garden, especially a secret one. British author Frances Hodgson Burnett knew this. Her bestselling classic *The Secret Garden* had at its horticultural heart a walled garden, the idea for which came from Burnett's own garden at Great Maytham Hall in England.

Walled gardens have always represented mystery, fantasy, romance and drama. Their secluded spaces, usually accessed by a solitary door cut into a high brick or stone wall, offer a private world hidden from outsiders, full of possibility and promise. They are unique, intimate spaces where colour, form and fragrance are concentrated.

In the south of London, in an area that feels beautifully rural even though it's still technically city, stands a walled garden that's reminiscent of Burnett's much-loved book; a garden that is the epitome of the word pleasure. The garden is part of a large 17th-century estate known as Petersham House, which itself is part of a cluster of grand estates scattered around Petersham Road in Richmond. It's a formidable concentration of opulence and architecture, but at its centre is something that's quite the opposite of grand: a charming sliver of garden that's barely bigger than a wheelbarrow.

Squeezed between Petersham House and its glasshouses – which have become famous as the backdrop for the whimsical, garden-themed tea room/café headed up by the culinary whiz Skye Gyngell – the walled garden is reached via a fabulous, atmospheric old iron gate and several brick steps. Push open this gate and you find yourself in a tiny paradise of earthy delights.

(Interestingly, the word 'paradise' is derived from an ancient Persian word meaning 'walled garden'.)

In one corner there is a long greenhouse, which looks much as a greenhouse should – slightly dilapidated but full of character and funny little plants and pots. In the back corner behind the greenhouse are the compost piles and the tool shed, which has a kind of industrial-chic feel. Then, filling the rest of the garden, grow a profusion of flowers and vegetables tumbling around structures and growing happily along walls.

Divided by a well worn brick path that invites you to explore, the garden doesn't have the formal plan or structure of a proper French potager, but is more of a traditional, utilitarian, Victorian-inspired kitchen garden with neat rows of produce and garden paraphernalia scattered around. There is also a collection of impressively large clay pots scattered throughout, and the garden grows around them in a delightfully rambling style.

But perhaps the most wonderful thing about the garden is the chook house, which is painted black and has big open wire windows. Here, contented-looking hens and a rooster cluck their way around the hay, sit on eggs or simply look out into the greenery around them. (Fortunately for them, the head chef often lets them out into the garden, believing that free chooks lay more delicious eggs, but it's uncertain what the head gardener, Lucy Boyd, thinks of this.)

What is most apparent about this kitchen garden is its sense of seclusion. It is truly a sanctuary. It is only accessible on two sides: by an ornate iron gate from the formal garden bordering the house, and by a simpler iron gate from the glasshouses and café. It is also usually off-limits to visitors, apart from annual Open Days, so the silence sits gently in the air. If you didn't know you were in London, you could be forgiven for thinking you were out in the middle of the English countryside.

Petersham House, its gardens and its business offshoot Petersham Nurseries are all owned by Gael and Francesco Boglione, who are so glamorous that magazines such as *Vogue* and *Harper's Bazaar* have devoted spreads to them, their family and their head chef Skye Gyngell. Gyngell has transformed the glasshouse café into a dazzling place to eat among the greenery and a cult Mecca for

London foodies – and she uses fresh produce from the walled garden in the café.

The place has been described as a 'bohemian idyll', but it is much more sophisticated than that. It is bohemian with a generous dash of grace and style.

Petersham House and Petersham Nurseries, with their quirky glasshouses and marvellous 'garden art', are truly inspirational places, but it is the tiny kitchen garden that is the real treasure here. It is a garden that Frances Hodgson Burnett would have been proud of.

Petersham Nurseries is open to the public seven days a week. Lunch in the café is available from Wednesday to Sunday, 12 pm to 2.45 pm. Reservations are essential (book as far ahead as possible). The walled kitchen garden is only open on select days throughout the year. Contact Petersham Nurseries or visit their website for details at www.petershamnurseries.com The café and nurseries are located on Church Lane, off Petersham Road, near Richmond, in Surrey (easily accessible by London tube to Richmond, and then a short taxi ride).

DESIGNING FOR A NARROW GARDEN

Long, narrow gardens can sometimes be difficult to design, unlike a square garden that can be divided easily into quadrants and sectioned off with crossed paths. To make the most of a long, narrow garden, try sectioning it into smaller gardens first. Do this by dividing it up with hedging, trellising, fencing or even espaliered fruit trees grown along a wire structure, which make beautiful dividers. Then plan your various areas between those sections. You can easily mark out a lawn, an entertaining terrace, a formal garden with a fountain, a vegetable patch or a flower garden. You can even have a potting shed, writer's retreat or chicken coop at the rear. All that's left is to link these sections with a long gravel path ribboning through the centre, and voila! The awkwardness of the narrow garden has gone. This kind of design also allows you to change some of these smaller gardens season by season, without destroying the beauty, integrity or planting schemes of the rest.

CREATING A WALLED GARDEN

You can create a secret garden, even on an urban block, by surrounding it with high hedges or walls. A simple picket fence with a pretty arbour and gate will also do the job.

ROYAL BOTANIC GARDENS

The greatest gift of the garden is the
restoration of the five senses.

HANNA RION

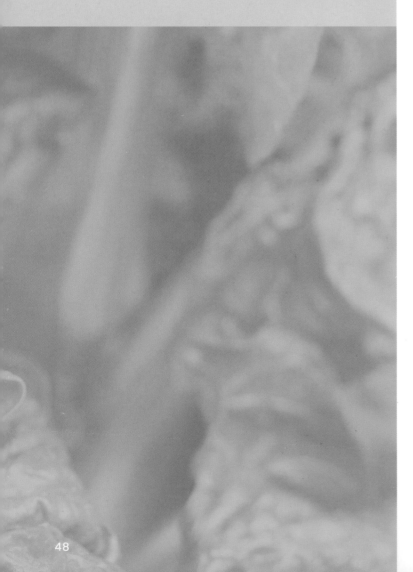

The Royal Botanic Gardens in Melbourne is one of the world's most beautiful botanic gardens. Situated in the heart of Melbourne, which is widely regarded as Australia's 'garden city' for its many beautiful parklands and green spaces, the Botanic Gardens is a reflection of how much this city loves its horticulture. On any given day, from glorious spring to foggy winter, you'll find people here: wandering the paths, jogging around the perimeter or picnicking beside one of the many lakes.

One of the most popular parts of the garden, especially with children, is the Ian Potter Foundation Children's Garden, a magical corner where the horticultural, educational, scientific, research and aesthetic elements of gardening collide in a splendid display of imagination.

The Ian Potter Foundation Children's Garden is divided into several gardens, among them a Ruin Garden, a Meeting Place (which has a water feature that sprays up out of the ground in summer), a Wetland Area, a Bamboo Forest, a Gorge, a Plant Tunnel and a Rill (a gentle waterway that runs through the garden). However, the most interesting part of this very hands-on space is the Kitchen Garden, which has been designed especially for kids. Built around a potting shed and a principal axis anchored by several tall bamboo wigwams, the garden consists of a dozen or so raised beds. In each of these beds, which sit at precisely the right height for little eyes to view their contents, are samples of some of the world's most unusual fruit, vegetables and herbs.

Children are encouraged to propagate plants in the potting shed with the help of horticultural staff, or simply dig in the dirt pit –

to the delight or dismay of their parents. (It's best to dress kids in their gumboots and garden clothes if you bring them here!)

With increasing urbanisation and high density living, there are fewer opportunities for children to venture outside to explore, experience and enjoy nature. With the help of the Ian Potter Foundation, this garden offers children a magical place to dig, build, hide, create and explore.

The Royal Botanic Gardens are open seven days a week, however the Ian Potter Foundation Children's Garden is closed for rest and maintenance from July to September each year. For details, visit www.rbg.vic.gov.au

INTEGRATING YOUR FLOWERS AND VEGETABLES

Integrated gardens have a long horticultural history. English Tudor kitchen gardens and French potagers were both forerunners of today's integrated kitchen gardens. Over time, the popularity of integrated gardens waned as people began to separate their vegetables from their flowers, and in fact shied away from vegetables altogether. In recent years, however, the integrated garden has had a horticultural renaissance as gardeners have come to realise that it not only saves space, which is often essential in small city residences, but also makes a garden more versatile and more appealing to be in. Mixing flowers and vegetables adds scent, height and colour to your garden and means that it puts on a vibrant show all year round. More importantly, integrated gardens optimise the health of your plants. Some flowers deter pests, while others attract bees and butterflies to help pollinate the garden. Nasturtiums and marigolds deter aphids and other pests, while tansy keeps away flying insects, Japanese beetles, striped cucumber beetles, squash bugs and even ants. Petunias, meanwhile, protect beans, while nettles keeps potato bugs away from potato crops.

Entrance

Grapefruit
and apple trees

Potting shed

Glasshouse

Citrus trees

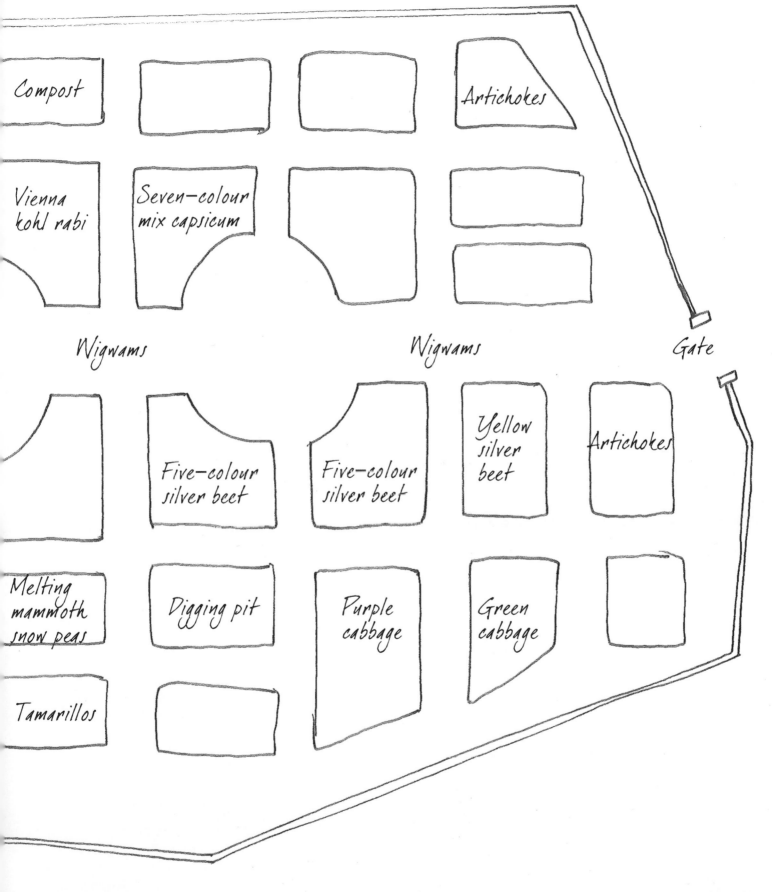

Compost

Artichokes

Vienna
kohl rabi

Seven-colour
mix capsicum

Wigwams

Wigwams

Gate

Five-colour
silver beet

Five-colour
silver beet

Yellow
silver
beet

Artichokes

Melting
mammoth
snow peas

Digging pit

Purple
cabbage

Green
cabbage

Tamarillos

CIRCA RESTAURANT

Shipping is a terrible thing to do to vegetables.
They probably get jet-lagged, just like people.

ELIZABETH BERRY

THE CHEF'S GARDEN

Like many chefs, Matt Wilkinson didn't relish the fact that his vegetables had to travel a significant distance before they reached his cutting board. He didn't like it that they were stuck in trucks, carted about on crates and left in dark rooms for days (even if they were refrigerated rooms). Matt wanted fresher vegetables – vegetables that had been picked just prior to preparation. He wanted vegetables that were so fresh that soil was still dangling from their roots. He just wasn't sure how to organise it.

Then he came up with an idea. He would plant a chef's garden – a garden that was located close to his restaurant so he could easily duck out and pick a handful of herbs or a basket of produce in between services. The only problem was location – where would he do it? The land around his restaurant, like most land in inner-city areas, was hundreds of thousands of dollars per square metre, which seemed a tad expensive for a kitchen garden.

At that stage, it seemed as if Matt's idea was dead before it had even been planted. But then Matt's boss – who owned the restaurant, and the hotel the restaurant was located in – stepped in and suggested the perfect solution.

The hotel was The Prince, the restaurant was Circa and the owner was John van Haandel. And the solution? A rooftop garden.

Now, both Circa and The Prince have always been known for being a little edgy, a little innovative. Their architecture and interior design is famous for consisting of one part glamour to three parts originality, and as such the place is beloved by the fashion and media crowds. So it wasn't much of a stretch to keep that edginess going – all the way up to the roof, in fact. To make the decision easier, Circa had recently undergone a design facelift that had seen the place emerge as a fresher, more energised space, so the rooftop garden was simply a continuation of the renovation – an exclamation mark at the end of a fabulous upgrade, if you like.

To design the garden, John van Haandel called in the equally edgy designer Joost Bakker, who has established a reputation for botanical art, architecture and interior design. Joost took one look at the architecture of The Prince and the height of the rooftop garden and decided to go up. Right up. As a result, his kitchen garden ended up being a vertical sculpture that matched the design and height of the building, rather than a traditional potager that would have wasted space on an already compact terrace.

The vertically stacked and tiered plant boxes, so reminiscent of library shelves, were an instant success. Matt filled them with soil and compost, and then planted as much as he could within their geometric borders, including globe artichokes, broad beans, white asparagus, fennel and radishes.

To complement this garden, Joost also designed a smaller, sister kitchen garden downstairs in a light-filled courtyard, which is home to a collection of herbs. This has the added benefit of making the dining courtyard smell wonderful!

The design of these kitchen gardens not only worked for the spaces they sat in, but they also perfectly suited Circa's cooking, which was – and still is – known for being innovative.

Matt Wilkinson has since left Circa to start his own restaurant, but the kitchen gardens remain. The new head chef, Jake Nicholson, adores them, and so do the diners.

Circa, 2 Acland Street, St Kilda, Melbourne.
Phone 03 9536 1122. www.circa.com.au

PROXIMITY TO THE KITCHEN

Try to locate your kitchen garden close to your kitchen. This will allow you easy access to the produce and herbs when you're preparing meals. There is nothing worse than positioning your kitchen garden at the far end of your backyard and then finding that you have to go all the way outside in the dark, navigating paths, steps, slugs and snails as you go, to pick a handful of mint for the roast. Circa's main rooftop garden may be situated on the top of the building, where it receives maximum sunlight, but it's sister herb garden is located downstairs in a pretty dining courtyard adjoining the kitchen. This smaller garden makes the job of retrieving herbs easy for the chefs and also makes the dining courtyard smell wonderful.

THE CHILDREN'S GARDEN

THE STEPHANIE ALEXANDER KITCHEN GARDEN FOUNDATION

Why try to explain miracles to your kids when you can just have them plant a garden?
ROBERT BRAULT

The suggestions that Stephanie Alexander offers to those who wish to join her Kitchen Garden Program are simple:

1 Stress pleasure, flavour and texture by encouraging conversation that uses all of the senses.
2 Do not use the word 'healthy' when describing food to children.
3 Expand children's vocabulary for food by encouraging them to describe flavours and textures, as well as plant families and names.
4 Try to come together around a table at the end of the cooking to share the meal.

Reading them, you can understand why this cook, restaurateur, author and all-round food guru is such a huge success. She understands food, but more importantly, she understands children and their tentative relationship with food – particularly healthy food. These suggestions make absolute sense, and yet seem to have been forgotten in this age of fast food, takeaway-bag-to-the-table dining.

Stephanie Alexander has come to be regarded as something of a gourmet goddess in recent years for her groundbreaking work in teaching children to eat through the use of her innovative kitchen garden program. Other chefs and food advocates such as Jamie Oliver are taking up the cause, but Stephanie Alexander was one of the first to insist on the importance of teaching children how to eat, and of showing them where their food comes from. A chef by trade, she started venturing into gardens when she noticed that children were ignorant of where vegetables came from. She instigated a program that put kitchen gardens into schools, and a decade on it has become a flourishing success. The Stephanie Alexander Kitchen Garden Program helps children to experience new foods, new flavours and new textures; to develop an appreciation of fresh, seasonal food; to develop new skills in the kitchen and garden that equip them to lead lives that are not dependent on processed foods; to develop their confidence and self-esteem; and, of course, to get out in the fresh air, enjoying physical activity. There are many other benefits too, such as an increased vocabulary in describing the various textures, tastes and sights they experience, developing social skills from eating around a table, and developing deeper understandings and tolerance of cultural difference by exposure to other culinary traditions. But the children don't even notice these things. All they really care about when they're out in the garden is whether the courgettes are ready to be picked and how the pumpkin tunnel is going.

At the Eaglehawk Primary School, near Bendigo in Victoria, it's easy to see how effective the Kitchen Garden Program is. The classes not only relish the opportunity to get out into the garden, but they also enjoy learning about horticulture and growing produce. They don't even mind working in the compost heap. There is a chook house, a hot house, a gourd tunnel, a water tank shaped like a watering can that pumps water when children ride the bike that's connected to it, lots of inspirational beds of vegetables, a fruit salad garden (more commonly known as an orchard) and of course the obligatory scarecrow.

The underlying belief of the Kitchen Garden Program is that by introducing this holistic approach to food, there is a chance of positively influencing children's food choices in new ways. In both

the kitchen and the garden the children work together in small groups with the help of volunteers. The finished dishes are arranged with pride and care on tables set with flowers from the garden, and the shared meal is a time for students, helpers, teachers and specialists to enjoy each other's company and conversation.

Further information about Stephanie Alexander's Kitchen Garden Foundation can be found at www.kitchengardenfoundation.org.au

ENCOURAGING CHILDREN TO GET THEIR HANDS DIRTY

Kids love getting out into the garden. To see the proof, you only need to watch their faces when you ask them to pick a basket of eggplants or walk through a gourd tunnel. They don't even mind composting. Encouraging children to plant and care for vegetables is not only important for their understanding of health, nutrition and where their food comes from, but also for their wellbeing. It allows them to get outside in the fresh air and get some exercise – and they usually don't even realise they're doing it! And there's nothing like harvesting vegetables (or in the case of some, particularly boys, sticking their hands into the dirt) to make kids happy.

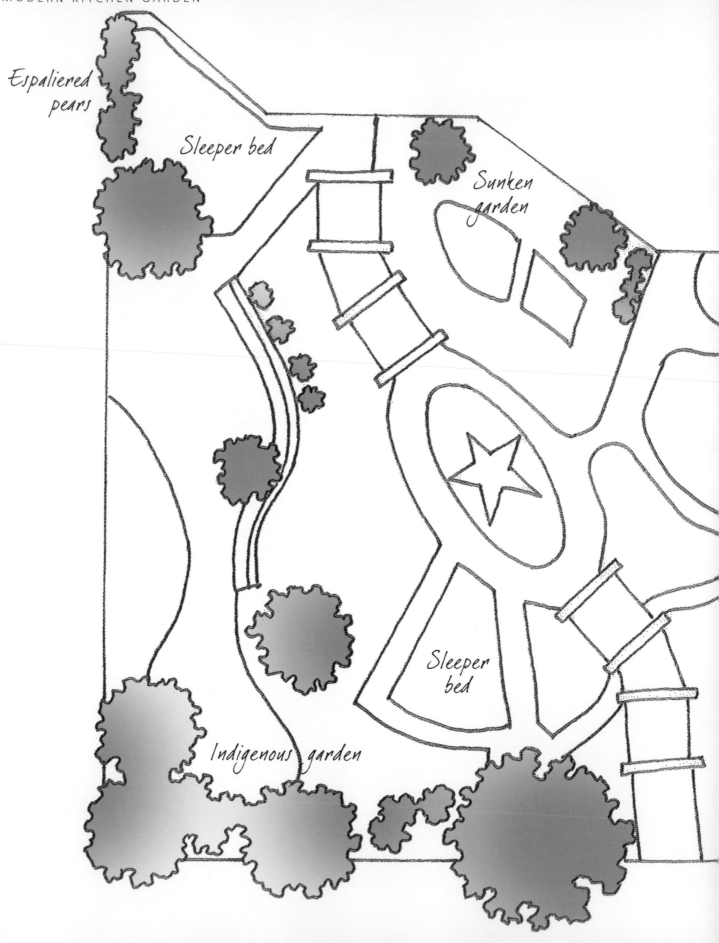

Espaliered pears

Sleeper bed

Sunken garden

Indigenous garden

Sleeper bed

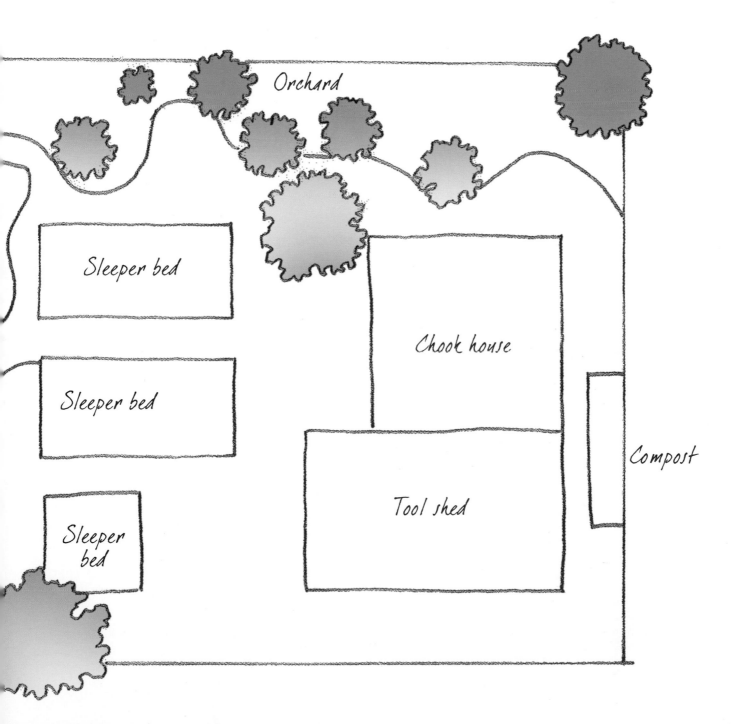

Orchard

Sleeper bed

Sleeper bed

Sleeper bed

Chook house

Tool shed

Compost

GLENMORE HOUSE

Gardens are not made by singing "Oh how beautiful" and sitting in the shade.

RUDYARD KIPLING

THE FAMILY GARDEN

If a country house is a great historian, then Glenmore House is surely an anthology of fabulous tales. A romantic, rambling sandstone house nestled in the Razorback Ranges about an hour's drive southwest of Sydney, it has been home to interior designer Mickey Robertson, her British-born husband Larry and their children since 1988.

During that time, the house has grown as much as the children, evolving from a tiny two-storey sandstone cottage with a handful of living areas and an attic bedroom to a handsome, spacious home, with two new wings and a gorgeous, distinctly Australian wraparound verandah. But while the house has undergone something of a growth spurt, it's the country garden that has really come of age.

Glenmore House's country garden is one of those gardens that you wish you owned – as long as you didn't have to do all the work to maintain it. It begins near an enchanting country gate at the back of the house, ambles around the verandah and courtyard with its Italian-style pots and gurgling fountain, then meanders around a former dairy, a lovely old barn, some stables, a fabulous old hayshed, a pool house and a charming potting shed, before tiptoeing down a set of stairs to a lower path, where it comes to a stop at an enormous kitchen garden. Garden designer Arne Maynard once wrote that 'a successful garden is one that has a sense of place, a perfect harmony between house, garden, history, owners and the surrounding landscape'. Glenmore House's garden has just that.

All credit for this must go to Mickey Robertson. When she and her husband first saw the property in 1988, it was just shy of being derelict. But when they took one look at the gentle yellow of the old sandstone cottage ('I mean look at it, how could you not fall in love?' she laughs), they couldn't resist. At that time, the house was barely liveable and the garden was little more than a few acres of dust with a view of the hills beyond, but that didn't deter Mickey. An interior designer by trade, she promptly went to work. She finished the original cottage in a year and set to work on the outbuildings and garden.

Noticing the close relationship between the garden and the various outbuildings, which are positioned fairly close together, she tried to integrate garden and architecture through paths, hedges, garden rooms and planting schemes so that the old buildings became an integral part of the beauty of the garden. She also worked hard to restore the old outbuildings.

She wanted the garden to be a place where family and visitors could explore, as well as feel at home; a place they could wander the paths, enjoy the scenes and shake their heads every time they turned a corner, ventured down steps or opened a gate and came across another of those marvellous pastoral views. Glenmore House's garden is testament to her vision and talents, but it is in the potager where Mickey Robertson's strengths are really evident.

This beautifully bucolic corner of the property is set on a lower elevation, behind the potting shed and dairy, which is now a

studio and lecture space for those students who come here to learn about growing vegetables. Mickey Robertson has converted what was once a slab of unused land into two flourishing kitchen gardens, filled with what are clearly happy vegies. Wherever possible, she seeks out heritage and organic varieties, and has planted everything from ruby Brussels sprouts and kale to Purple Podded Dutch Peas.

Such has been her success in this kitchen garden – although she freely admits there has also been a lot of 'trial and error' – that Mickey started to wonder whether others might be interested in learning how to create their own vegetable gardens, so she and garden expert Linda Ross set up a series of courses. They sold out before you could say 'seed raising'.

Mickey Robertson runs regular kitchen garden days in her country garden at Glenmore House, near Camden, south of Sydney. For details, visit www.glenmorehouse.com.au or email mickey@glenmorehouse.com.au

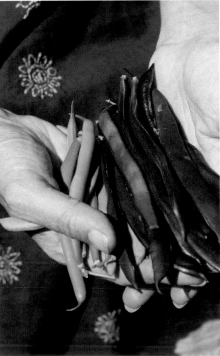

EXPERIMENTING WITH VEGETABLES

When it comes to choosing seeds for your vegetable garden, don't be afraid to experiment. It's wonderful to fall back on the old favourites – corn, tomatoes, lettuces and so on – but it's also rather exciting to think outside the square (or the vegetable garden) to see what other kinds there are. The dark-chocolate-coloured Sweet Chocolate Capsicum, for example, looks fabulous growing in a garden, and even more amazing sliced up in salads. (And it tastes delicious!) The *Listada de Gandia* is one of the most beautiful eggplant varieties available today, bearing gorgeous purple and white striped fruits that taste just as lovely as they look. *Rosa Bianca* eggplants are also pretty, with their purple and white skin, while the Casper Eggplant grows curious, ghostly white eggplants that taste a little like mushrooms.

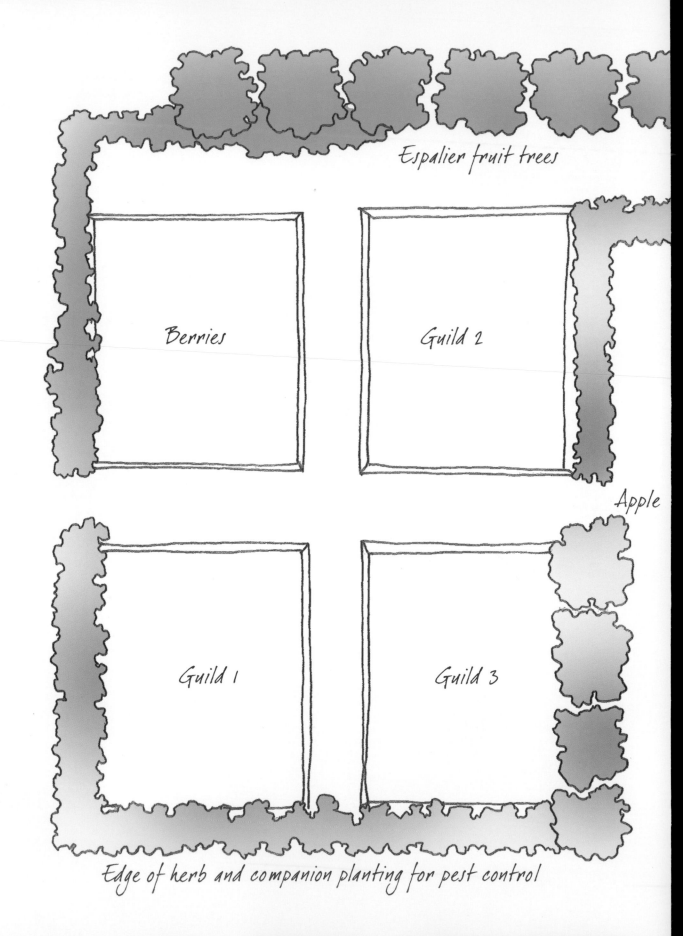

Espalier fruit trees

Berries

Guild 2

Apple

Guild 1

Guild 3

Edge of herb and companion planting for pest control

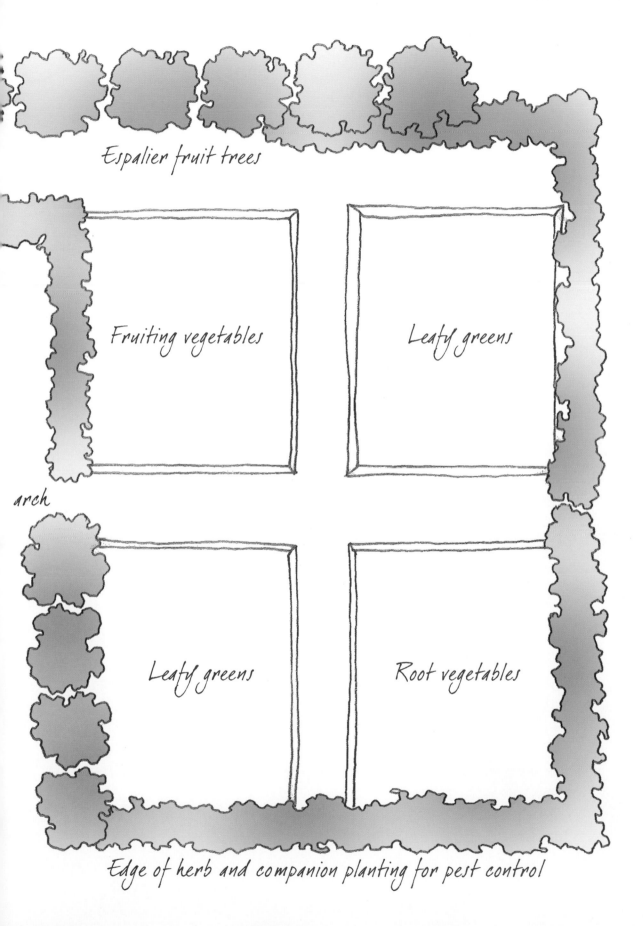

Espalier fruit trees

Fruiting vegetables

Leafy greens

arch

Leafy greens

Root vegetables

Edge of herb and companion planting for pest control

LONDON ALLOTMENT

There is no such thing as a little garlic.
ARTHUR BAER

THE FOOD CRITIC'S GARDEN

Y ou'd drive right past it if you didn't know it was there. Tucked away behind a line of bushy hedges and accessed via a narrow gravel road, it hints at a world unseen by most, a Lewis Carollesque Wonderland of colour, scent and delight. It also promises a refuge from the raucous pace of the city, and that alone is enough to entice most visitors inside.

It's an allotment, a wondrously large one, and it's one of hundreds dotted throughout urban London – most of them hidden just as well as this one. Enter through the locked gate (only those with an allotment have a key) and you step into a pastoral realm right in the middle of the city. Blink and you'd think you were in Kent, passing through a country garden.

Allotments have become big news in London in recent years, mostly because they're becoming an endangered species. According to a recent study carried out by the London Assembly, more than 1500 plots have been lost in London over the past 10 years, which is an area roughly the size of 50 football pitches. There are now only 737 allotment sites remaining, encompassing a total of more than 20,000 individual garden plots. The ironic thing is that while these coveted sites are being bulldozed over by property developers and councils looking for more land to accommodate the city's growing population, the popularity of the allotments has soared. Demand for allotments has never been higher, thanks to the growing interest in organic food. More than 4300 people are on London's allotment waiting lists – some 3000 more than a decade ago. In some cases the wait is 10 years or more.

So why the passion for these old-fashioned plots? Well, according to Mr Hulme-Cross from the Allotments Regeneration Initiative, the benefits of allotments are two-fold. There is the health aspect – namely, being outside, engrossed in physical labour, then driving home with a basket full of just-plucked, home-grown vegies. Then there is the community aspect, which is something people seem to love just as much as the gardening itself. 'Allotments bring so many benefits, including strong social networks, the health and financial advantages of growing fresh produce, and a real sense of community,' says Mr Hulme-Cross.

Two people who know all about allotments are Neil and Angela Davey, a husband-and-wife team who love nothing more than to escape to their private patch of land on weekends and do a bit of weeding. Neil Davey is a London-based restaurant critic and food writer who has a hugely popular blog (thelambshankredemption.blogspot.com), which was recently voted among the best food blogs by London's *Telegraph* newspaper. He loves food, naturally, but the plot was actually his wife Angela's idea. She thought it would be a wonderful way to access fresh vegetables while spending time together. Now, she spends more time than he does in the garden, but he reciprocates by cooking up a storm with the produce they bring home.

Their plot is fairly large by allotment standards – 9 metres by 33 metres (most allotments are smaller because of land restrictions) – and features a spacious 'greenhouse' (plastic for now, but the Daveys have plans for bigger things). Their allotment may be large but their neighbours' plots are even grander: two

gentlemen have created magnificent garden oases complete with neat, weed-free paths, sophisticated-looking scarecrows and shabby-chic sheds.

Like many virgin allotment holders, the Daveys made the mistake during their first year of ownership of becoming caught up in the excitement of having fresh produce, and planted everything they could think of. The following year, exhausted from the work, they pared the beds back to plump strawberries, rosy potatoes and pungent-smelling garlic – that is, says Neil Davey, much more delicious than store-bought garlic. (It also

smells twice as strong, which is perhaps why it's so much more effective in food.)

They haven't organised the beds, paths and design in a coherent fashion quite yet, but it's coming along, and it's easy to see that it's an ongoing process of labour and love. You can also see the sheer pleasure in their eyes when they're pulling out the weeds, assessing crops or simply tucking into a strawberry or three. With the spring sun shining down, butterflies flitting through the grass and the scent of fresh garlic in the air, there couldn't be a better place to be anywhere in north London.

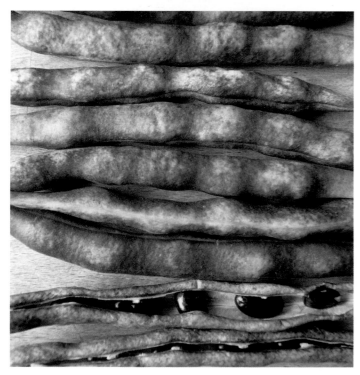

CHOOSE YOUR VEGETABLES WITH CARE

A common mistake many people make when they're planting their first kitchen garden is to go crazy with the quantities of vegetables they grow. They become caught up in exotic varieties and romantic names. Purple heirloom carrots? Fabulous! White cucumbers and yellow cauliflower? Let's buy the seeds now! Halfway through the first year, and exhausted from trying to keep it all together, they realise they don't really eat a lot of carrots, and perhaps don't even like the taste of cauliflower, and they sure as heck don't know how to cook a white cucumber. The second year, they realise they just want a few potatoes, some leeks and onions and perhaps a pumpkin or two for the Sunday roast. Suddenly, life in the garden becomes a lot easier.

The first rule of planning and planting a kitchen garden is to only plant what you want to eat. Sure, *Listada de Gandia* eggplants look pretty but if you don't like the taste, they're a waste of good soil space. Work out what you eat regularly and try to plant those vegetables as a priority. If you have space leftover, then plant the more unusual varieties. By all means experiment with seeds, but if you start to fail, or find your baskets are full of things you don't know what to do with, you'll soon become disheartened and give up on gardening altogether.

A garden is a grand teacher.

GERTRUDE JEKYLL

THE FORMAL GARDEN

To discover a country estate as grand, as green and as formal as Larundel in the middle of the otherwise dry Australian bush is a bit of a shock. It rises out of the native landscape like an oasis; a relic of a colonial time when country estates had more water – and perhaps also more staff bustling about to maintain them. There are dignified avenues of Manchurian pear and Chinese poplar trees, hedge-lined garden 'rooms', spectacular courtyards with classical fountains and urns and even enchanting pear walks. Blink and you'd think you'd been transported to an English estate.

The elegant 1870 Victorian mansion and its garden, which is part of a larger 4000-acre pastoral estate established in the late 1800s by the Austin family, is owned by the Preat family who moved here from Melbourne when they fell in love with the rural scene. The spectacular state of the house and garden is the result of the hard work of both the Preat family and the former owner, Craig Kimberley, as well as two designers who injected their extraordinary talent and creativity into the interior and grounds: the world-renowned, London-based interior designer John Coote and the noted Australian garden designer Paul Bangay. Interestingly, the garden was one of Bangay's first commissions and it displays all the signature features of his classical designs, including precise angles, perfect symmetry, strong sight lines and rich detail.

Both the house and the garden are spectacular, but it is the garden than really enchants. The design features 10 formal garden 'rooms', each defined by hedges of glossy-leafed holly that are clipped to frame the views of the landscape beyond. The central axis of the design is a series of descending terraces that tumble, in staircase-style, from the higher elevation behind the house to the lower level in front of the house. At its lowest point, this principal axis is crossed by another main axis, a rather poetic path that begins at the house and then passes through various gardens, including a lovely allée bordered by Chinese poplars, before finishing at The Long Walk, where it is elegantly ended by an antique urn from Lord McAlpine's English estate at West Green. (The Long Walk, which links the garden to the grasslands beyond, runs perpendicular to this romantic allée and parallel to the first axis.)

These three grand axes, which together form a 'U' shape, are balanced by several secondary cross-axes that connect the series of garden rooms scattered between them. The total effect is a kind of horticultural order, a disciplined framework of garden, gravel paths, clipped hedges and spectacular country views.

There is something intense and compelling about the absoluteness of the execution. But despite the fiercely disciplined lines, or perhaps because of them, Larundel is a garden of harmony, romance and calm that prompts reflection and repose.

One of the most popular rooms in the entire garden is the potager, which is adored by the Preat's two children, Will and Tiffany. Situated in the top corner of the garden, this fascinating potager is bordered by the same formal hedges as the rest of the garden rooms, which creates a sense of mystery and intrigue. It's still within sight of the homestead and the old kitchen wing though,

and from inside you can see the fireplaces peeking over the top of the hedges.

Designed along the lines of a formal French potager, the garden is centred round a tree trimmed into a delightful topiary cone. Around this tree there are several gravel paths that run in a geometric fashion, following the square lines of the hedged perimeter. Placed into this design are several miniature hedge-bordered beds that are designed to mirror the taller perimeter hedges, but on a much smaller scale. Inside these hedged beds, the estate's gardeners have planted all manner of

produce, ranging from Swiss chard and rhubarb to strawberries and chives.

Set between these hedged beds there are also several raised beds that are planted with a profusion of flowers and produce. And scattered among it all is a fantastic collection of unusual garden architecture, ranging from vintage iron bed heads embedded between the vegetables and the perimeter hedges to create a sculptural divide, to old metal grates that have been used as gates.

The effect of the potager, taken as a whole, is a little like stumbling onto a secret garden: unexpected but thoroughly wonderful.

Larundel is a private estate, but it is open to the public on select open days throughout the year. For details on Larundel, see www.larundelestate.com

CREATING A FORMAL GARDEN IN A SMALL SPACE

The Preat's potager is a beautiful example of how you can create a formal kitchen garden in a relatively small space, thanks to hedging, a clever, disciplined geometric garden design and careful plantings. Even though the elements are formal, everything is done on a small scale, making it seem grand and yet intimate at the same time. Even a 2-metre-square plot can have a formal feel. Simply use box hedging for borders (both outside and inside the kitchen garden), design the garden around a formal framework – diamonds or a cross – and then plant and clip into shape small topiary-style trees at the edges and centre.

INTEGRATING ORNAMENTATION

The Preats own a staggeringly impressive collection of priceless garden art, including a huge garden urn from the Rothschild estate in France that was sourced through Sotheby's, but they've also introduced lots of inexpensive and quirky pieces, such as vintage iron bed heads. Garden art is a clever way of elevating your garden from a green space into a gallery of sculpture, texture, materials and form, and the quirkiest of man-made pieces can sit easily amid the best of Mother Nature. Simply design the garden around a formal framework by using a cross or quadrant pattern with four beds, and then use box hedging for borders (both outside and inside the kitchen garden). You can also add ornamentation such as a small square fountain, an urn, topiary or an obelisk to give a formal feel to a small garden.

VILLANDRY

Gardeners, I think, dream bigger dreams
than Emperors.
MARY CANTWELL

THE GRAND CHÂTEAU GARDEN

Ah, the Château de Villandry. What can one say about the Taj Mahal of kitchen gardens? A Mecca for gardeners the world over, Villandry inspires the same glassy-eyed reverence that St Andrews does for golfers, Goodwood does for car lovers and New York does for architects. It is an unparalleled space of line, form, greenery, symmetry, detail, drama and garden art that lifts gardening to a whole other level. To try to describe it is like trying to describe, well, heaven on earth really. All you can do is look around and say, 'oh my ...'.

To really appreciate the majesty of Villandry, you need to get up high. A hot air balloon is the best elevation from which to view this garden, but if you can't manage that, then the tower of Villandry's château or the nearby belvedere terrace are the next best things. From here, you can see the garden in its entirety and really appreciate the scale of the design. It is, quite simply, extraordinary.

Designed in an intricate pattern of nine geometric squares, each of them edged in immaculately clipped boxwood, Villandry's potager is visual poetry. It may not seem like genius to plant nine garden squares with more than 40 types of vegetables, arranged according to colour, form and companion planting rules, but when you get up high and look out over the potager, it's easy to see why people make the trek here from all over the world. The entire garden looks as if it was painted, rather than planted, with the tight lines of cabbages, radishes, lettuces, chard and celery resembling broad brushes dipped in paint pots of French gray, pale green, fuchsia and chartreuse. No two of the nine squares are alike, but together they form an artwork of intensity and luminosity that is like nothing else on earth.

The idea for the magnificent potager came from the great-grandfather of the château's current owner. Dr Joachim Carvallo was a former scientist who fell in love with Villandry in 1906 and purchased it with his American-born wife, Ann Coleman. Dr Carvallo then left his scientific profession in order to save the château, which was about to be demolished, and devote himself to its gardens. Over the next few decades, he poured enormous amounts of energy, time and money into the property. Using as his guide the geometric principles of design perfected by André LeNôtre, who created the royal gardens for Louis XIV at Versailles, he created a garden that is in complete harmony with the Renaissance architecture of the château. Many people now consider it one of the most beautiful gardens in the world.

There are many extraordinary things about Villandry's potager, including its scale and its design, the crosses of which cleverly evoke the monasteries of the Middle Ages – there are even roses between the squares to represent the monks who once tended such gardens. But perhaps the most amazing thing about the potager is its planting scheme. In keeping with its historic design, Villandry's nine squares are only planted with vegetables that were grown in this region in the 1500s. This means that some of today's most common and popular vegetables are absent – there are no tomatoes or potatoes, for example. All of the squares are dug up and replanted each season. That's a total of 60,000 historic vegetables each year, a figure that is all the more astonishing considering that there are only eight gardeners who work full-time here, and they have the rest of the château's gardens to consider, too (another 45,000 plants). As well as the

potager, Villandry's gardens encompass a water garden, which is similar in spirit to those of Versailles, a Garden of Love, a Garden of Music, a herb garden, a topiary garden and several other beautiful green spaces, all of which reflect the same harmony, beauty and refined style of the potager.

But while the entire property is astonishing (Château de Villandry was designated a *monument historique* in 1934, and like all the other châteaux of the Loire Valley is a World Heritage Site), it is the potager that is perhaps the most popular part of this glamorous garden.

Villandry was one of the first places to showcase the beauty of ornamental vegetables, and to show that purple and green cabbages, ruby chard and coloured lettuces could become horticultural art. It is still one of the world's grandest and best-loved gardens.

Château de Villandry is located in the Loire Valley of France and is open seven days a week. For details, visit www.chateauvillandry.fr

WHY BORDERS AND ARCHITECTURE ARE AS IMPORTANT AS PRODUCE

When many enthusiastic gardeners begin planting their kitchen gardens, they often concentrate on the plants and produce and forget about borders and framework, which is a little like decorating the interior of a house when you haven't yet erected the walls and architecture. A good kitchen garden design involves well-thought-out structure and framework as much as it does soil, seeds, fertilizer, sun and water. Structure gives a garden a skeleton to hang on, and provides horticultural boundaries so that the plants don't end up wandering aimlessly all over the place. It is the architecture around which the garden grows. It can also give the garden height and visual form. Villandry's magnificent potager is beautiful because it is enclosed with a spectacularly patterned framework of highly ordered box hedge borders. These borders are regularly clipped so they remain at a low height, and this allows the colours and textures of the produce to be seen from afar, or a great height (such as atop the chateau). The potager is as much about the borders as it is about the produce within those borders. Smaller kitchen gardens can use the same principles as Villandry by utilizing borders made from box hedge, wattling, bricks or simple timber sleepers. These will not only neatly enclose the soil and plants within but also give the garden definition, boundaries and structure.

Allium fistulosum
Ciboule

A vegetable garden in the beginning looks
so promising and then after all little by little
it grows nothing but vegetables …
nothing but vegetables.

GERTRUDE STEIN

THE HEIRLOOM GARDEN

It was bound to happen. As the world became caught up in the kitchen garden revival and started rediscovering the flavour of fresh vegetables, it was only a matter of time before people started searching for more unusual and rare varieties to plant and cook with. Enter the heirloom vegetable.

Heirloom vegetables have been around for a number of years, but their popularity just keeps growing and growing, helped in part by curious gardeners eager to see what a Royalty Purple Pod Bean looks like (supposedly one of the most beautiful vegetables ever), and even more curious chefs eager to see what it tastes like (not as good as it looks).

For those not *au fait* with heirloom plants, an heirloom vegetable is one that was commonly grown during earlier periods in human history but that is not grown today in commercial quantities. There is some debate about what actually constitutes an 'heirloom' vegetable – some people think it should be those vegetables that are 100 years old, and others believe it should be those that were grown before 1945 (which marks the end of the Second World War and the beginning of widespread use of hybrids by growers and seed companies, and industrial agriculture). Still other gardeners consider 1951 to be the latest a plant can have originated and still be called an heirloom, since that year marked the widespread commercial introduction of the hybrid varieties.

It is thought that more than 2000 heirloom vegetables have been lost since the 1970s. This figure fluctuates depending on who you're speaking to, but what is clear is that there seem to be far fewer varieties of vegetables around in supermarkets today than there were even 20 years ago.

Many organisations are trying to change that. The United States-based non-profit Seed Savers Exchange (www.seedsavers.org) is one. Vaucluse House is another.

Vaucluse House is a spectacularly beautiful historic property in Sydney's eastern suburbs. It is one of Sydney's best-preserved and most authentic 19th-century homes. The house itself is worth visiting (the historic kitchen is extraordinary), but it's the kitchen garden that many people are flocking to. A decade or so ago, the custodians of Vaucluse House (the Historic Houses Trust) decided to re-establish the kitchen garden as part of the ongoing restoration of the historic property. It was also planned to provide insight into the lives and eating habit of our forebears.

Every effort was made to preserve the authenticity of the garden by researching newspapers and references of the time to determine garden designs of the period, and of course, heirloom varieties of vegetables were used. Head gardener David Gray also improved the soil so that it would be more receptive to the new types of heirloom seeds. Because the house is situated near the coast the soil is predominantly sandy, so lots of mulch had to be incorporated into the soil, as well as blood and bone and superphosphate.

Since the 19th-century kitchen garden was reinstated, Vaucluse has made pumpkins and parsnips into hot property. While the garden may not be as big as it was in its heyday a century or so ago, it still has the power to pack a horticultural punch.

Vaucluse House is open to the public from Friday to Sunday. (It is open daily during January.) For details, visit www.hht.net.au/museums/vaucluse_house

HEIRLOOM VEGETABLES: THE HEIGHT OF HORTICULTURAL FASHION

Violetta di Firenze eggplant, Spanish Roja garlic, Brandywine tomatoes, *Ronde de Nice* squash, Blue Lake beans, Lemon cucumbers and Bulgarian carrots… These deliciously named vegetables are all heirloom vegetables. And they're the hottest things in horticulture since, well, the chilli. Heirloom vegetables have become rather fashionable in the last decade, prized as much for their flavour as for the fact that they're easy to grow. There's something about the taste of these endearing vegies that reminds you of the old-fashioned kind your grandmother used to grow. The tomatoes taste like real tomatoes. The corn tastes like it did when you were a child. And the eggplants! Oh! While people can't agree on what precisely constitutes an heirloom variety (the age of the cultivar is a much-discussed topic), everyone agrees that they're worth growing. There are, however, some issues with heirlooms. Like anything old, they have their quirky traits. Some seeds germinate slower than their modern counterparts, and some may be more susceptible to disease. Then, when they finally do grow, they may do so as upside-down vegetables. Some appear to struggle, then pop up when you least expect them to. And others – like all plants – may not be suited to the conditions in your back yard. But all these quirks are part of the endearing charm of heirlooms.

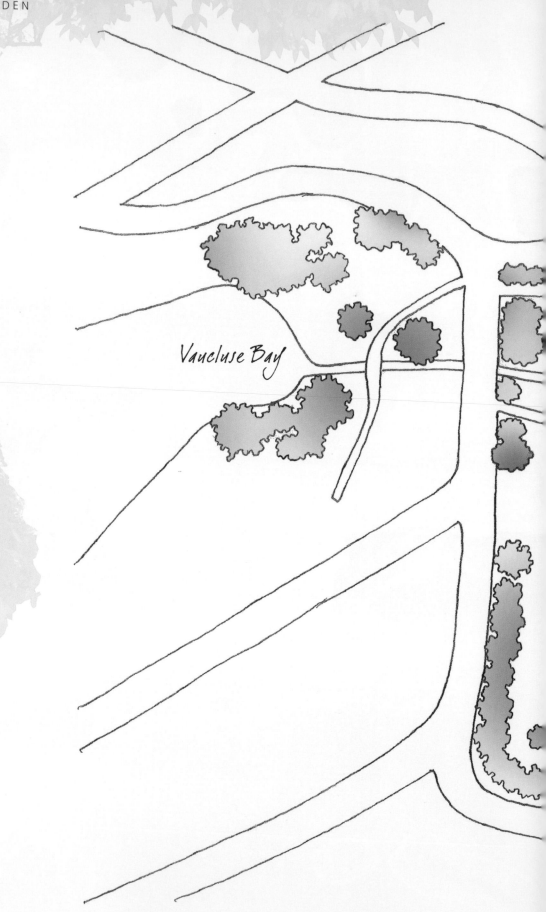

Vaucluse Bay

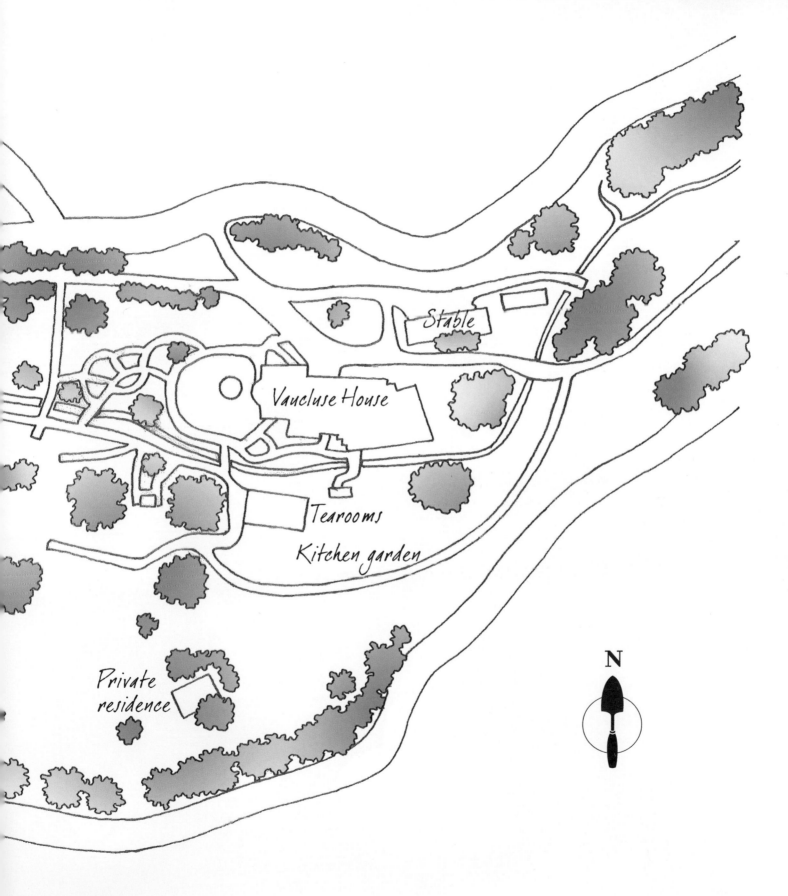

Stable

Vaucluse House

Tearooms

Kitchen garden

Private
residence

N

THE HISTORIC GARDEN

COMO HOUSE

There is nothing that is comparable, as satisfactory, or as thrilling as gathering the vegetables one has grown.
ALICE B. TOKLAS

Como House has long been on the list of historic places for Melbourne school children to visit as one of their annual excursions, and is loved by littlies as much for its interiors (ghosts, strange noises and mysterious initials etched into windows) as its exteriors (old kitchens, laundries and glorious rambling gardens).

Built in 1847, it's an intriguing mix of Australian Regency and classic Italianate architecture. The house's name supposedly comes from Lake Como in Italy, which is where the first owner, Edward Eyre Williams, proposed to his wife Jessie Gibbon. A member of Melbourne's colonial elite, Mr Williams entertained lavishly at Como before deciding he didn't like it and selling it to investor Frederick Dalgety in 1852. Less than a year later, Mr Dalgety sold it to Scotsman John Brown and his wife Helen, who added to the architecture of the house by commissioning a second story, tower and new outbuildings. The Browns also commissioned the renowned gardener William Sangster to transform the grounds into five acres of breathtaking gardens. However, the Browns went bankrupt, so in 1864 Como House was sold yet again, this time to Charles Armytage, who, with his wife Caroline, raised 10 children here. The Armytage family remained at Como for over 95 years, until they handed it over to the National Trust in 1959.

All of these owners contributed to the glamour, grandeur and myths surrounding Como House — and possibly to the ghosts, too. Today, it stands as a glorious snapshot of Victorian history, and a magnificent example of Melbourne architecture.

The grand formal rooms, bedrooms and gorgeous colonial verandah are among the most popular parts of the house, however there is another just-as-beautiful part of Como that exists in a corner of the estate that most people miss completely. It's the newly restored kitchen garden, and it's a classic example of a colonial kitchen garden from the turn of the century.

Created after 1911, the garden had to cater for the household's many family members and servants. It was abandoned after the war due to a lack of staff to tend to it, and subsequently fell into decline. Years later, when the National Trust decided to restore the garden to its former glory as part of the Federation celebrations, they set about excavating it and slowly revived the old kitchen garden.

According to gardener Dugald Noyes who was working at Como at the time of the garden revival (he is now at Heide), the original layout of the garden was discovered from an old 1940s aerial photo, which showed the rows of vegetables planted out in an east–west orientation. Digital technology was used to overlay the 1945 aerial photo onto a 1999 site survey – this enabled the dimensions of the garden to be determined with reasonable accuracy.

Seed catalogues dating back to the 1920s were used to choose the vegetables to be grown in the kitchen garden at Como, and the beds were cultivated using traditional companion planting methods. Now the garden is thriving once again, just as it did in the 1900s.

Como House & Garden is open at varying times throughout the year. To check the latest open times, visit www.comohouse.com.au

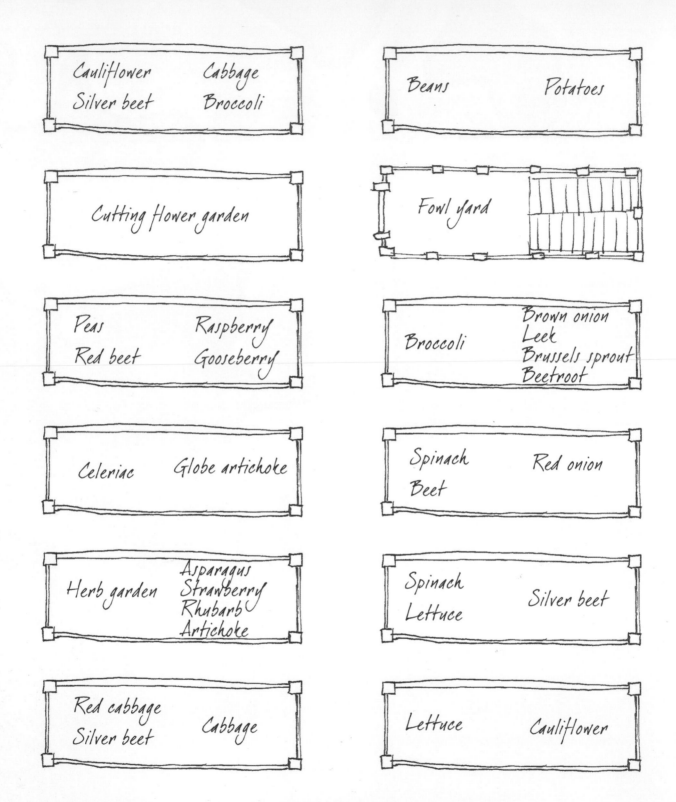

Cauliflower   Cabbage
Silver beet   Broccoli

Beans   Potatoes

Cutting flower garden

Fowl yard

Peas   Raspberry
Red beet   Gooseberry

Broccoli   Brown onion
                     Leek
                     Brussels sprout
                     Beetroot

Celeriac   Globe artichoke

Spinach   Red onion
Beet

Herb garden   Asparagus
               Strawberry
               Rhubarb
               Artichoke

Spinach
Lettuce   Silver beet

Red cabbage
Silver beet   Cabbage

Lettuce   Cauliflower

COMO KITCHEN GARDEN

July 2009

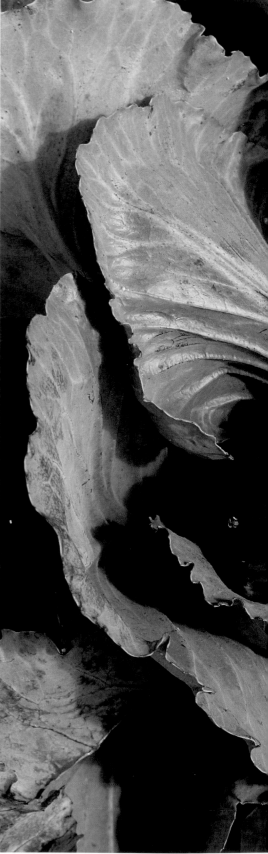

LE POTAGER DU ROI

The best way to get real enjoyment out of the garden is to put on a wide straw hat, hold a little trowel in one hand and a cool drink in the other, and tell the man where to dig.

CHARLES BARR

THE KING'S GARDEN

It takes a certain amount of perseverance to see inside the great *Potager du Roi*, or the Kitchen Garden of the King, at the Palace of Versailles. I had to return to Versailles three times before I finally gained access. The entrance is also rather difficult to find, so unless you're dedicated, you may end up giving up and going to find a cosy café somewhere on the Rue de Satory to fortify yourself with a strong espresso and a *tarte tartin*. But to do so would be a tragedy worthy of Marie Antoinette, because the *Potager du Roi* is a potager worth seeing.

This stupendously grand kitchen garden (it's almost a tautology but really, there are no other words for it) was created in 1678 to supply fresh fruit and vegetables to King Louis XIV and his immediate and extended royal family, which at the time numbered more than 300. Now, 300 people is no small number to serve meals to. (This didn't include the 1000 to 10,000 people who needed to be fed in the King's Court!) But add to that the fact that in Versailles at this time, they didn't exactly believe in petit salads, and you start to realise just how much food was going back and forth here. Meals would have been feasts, so the kitchens would have needed to be stuffed with ingredients.

Enter the *Potager du Roi*.

Originally part of the greater Versailles estate, the potager was designed by the great landscape architect Jean-Baptiste La Quintinie, who trained as a lawyer before becoming passionate about plants. Construction took five years, from 1678 to 1683, and required hundreds of workers because the site was originally swampland, and not at all suitable for growing produce. (It was

known as *l'etang puant*, or 'the stinking pond'.) After it was drained and filled in, the renowned architect Mansart constructed the garden's terraces and walls. La Quintinie then did the rest.

The original garden covered 25 acres, and was designed around a central circular pond and fountain. Around this pond was *le Grand Carré*, or 'the Grand Square', which was made up of 16 smaller garden squares.

Surrounding *le Grand Carré* was a high wall, and behind the wall were a further 29 enclosed gardens featuring fruit trees and vegetables. There were also raised terraces, on which King Louis XIV could watch the gardeners work. Are you starting to get an idea of how gargantuan this garden was now?

Much of this magnificent framework is still standing, albeit without the bustling gardeners, and it still produces an impressive amount of fruit and vegetables, perhaps more fruit than in the 17th century.

In Louis's time, the garden included hundreds of different types of fruit and vegetables, including 50 varieties of pears, 20 varieties of apples and 16 different varieties of lettuce for the king's table. It also featured a *figuerie* (a sheltered fig garden), a special melon garden, three separate herb gardens and gardens reserved for strawberries and cherries.

Today, the actual shape of the potager is much the same as it was three centuries ago, however the varieties of fruit and vegetables grown have changed slightly. Included in the modern selection are gourds, pear-shaped tomatoes, 'kilometre' beans, Jerusalem artichokes and other unusual vegetables.

But while the varieties may have changed, the gardeners still like to remember King Louis XIV by growing produce he was fond of, such as *Bezy de la Motte* pears. He also loved figs and strawberries. His favourite food, however, was the legendary *Téton de Vénus*, or the 'Tit of Venus', a peach that apparently tasted simply divine.

Le Potager du Roi is still an extraordinary place, and you can easily imagine what it would have been like during the height of its activity. Even the grand gate to the palace is still there – look for it on the side opening to the *Allée du Potager* and the *Pièce d'Eau des Suisses*.

The Potager du Roi is located at 10 Rue du Marechal Joffre in Versailles, and is open on certain days. In winter (January to March) it is usually Tuesdays and Thursdays. From March onwards, it is usually Tuesday to Sunday. However, check the website for the most up-to-date details. There are guided tours available, but these may be in French. For more details, visit www.potager-du-roi.fr

USING SPACE TO CREATE

The King's Garden at Versailles is kitchen gardening on a truly grand scale. Not all of us have 25 acres spare to devote to vegetable growing, but there are a lucky few – usually those who live in the country – who do have room, and who want to know how to use it wisely. If you live in acreage, or even on half an acre, and don't know how to make the most of it, take a tip from La Quintine. Firstly, section your garden into manageable areas. Find a nice square spot in which to position the kitchen garden, preferably close to the house and particularly the kitchen. Turn the middle section into a central showpiece garden, perhaps set around a fountain or urn. (You can always create a patterned parterre from box hedge and fill it with herbs.) If there's an awkward area at the back of your garden that receives plenty of sun, turn it into a delightful orchard. Consider fencing it off from the rest of the garden – then you can put a small chicken coop in there and let the chickens roam around the orchard during the day. Fruit trees hate grass and love chicken manure, so it's a win–win situation. And if there's a long, narrow area that you don't know how to use, consider turning it into a pear walk. Look at the kitchen garden at Versailles for inspiration, and copy some of the design elements into your smaller acreage garden.

Balbi Parc

Les Onze

Duhamel du Monceau
Garden

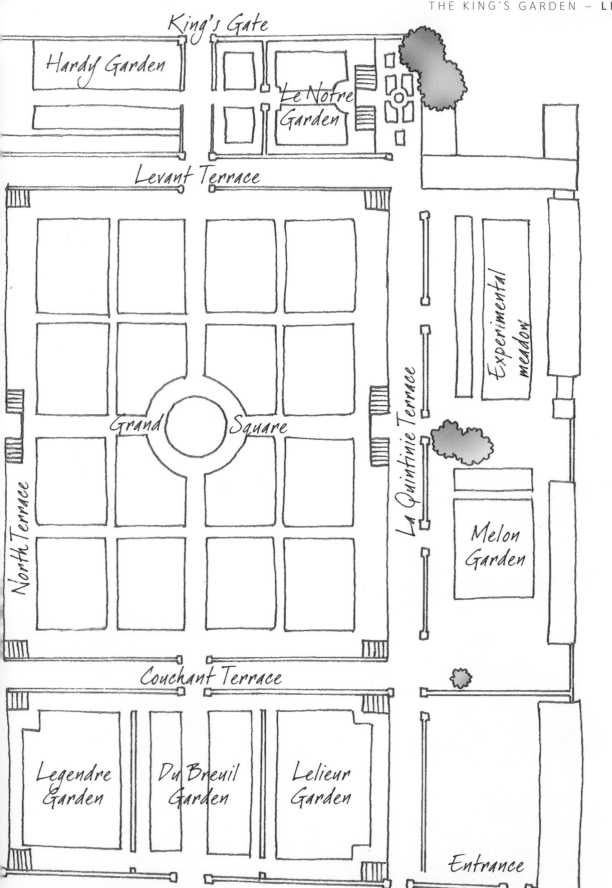

King's Gate

Hardy Garden

Le Nôtre Garden

Levant Terrace

North Terrace

Grand Square

La Quintinie Terrace

Experimental meadow

Melon Garden

Couchant Terrace

Legendre Garden

Du Breuil Garden

Lelieur Garden

Entrance

THE ORGANIC GARDEN

When Daylesford Organic exhibited at the Chelsea Flower Show in 2008, their kitchen garden exhibit, delightfully dubbed 'Summer Solstice', was one of the most visited gardens at the show. It wasn't simply because Daylesford Organic is one of England's most talked-about gourmet food brands. It was reflecting the growing trend for people to grow their own food by creating edible, organic gardens. It was also one of the most inspirational gardens ever shown at Chelsea.

The exhibition garden, conceived by Daylesford Organic's Lady Bamford and designed by Del Buono Gazerwitz, comprised a miniature wheat field reaching maturity, a walled kitchen garden planted with vegetables and herbs enclosed by woven willow and a contemporary 'garden kitchen' structure in which produce from the garden could be prepared. It was intended to be a snapshot of the picturesque Daylesford Organic farm in the Cotswolds and a reflection of the company's philosophy and belief in gardening in harmony with nature, but it ended up being far more than that. Carole Bamford called it an 'organic agrarian garden for the new century'.

No one had ever done a wheat field for Chelsea before, and few had tried kitchen gardens. But 'Summer Solstice' was perfect, complete with wildlife-friendly wildflowers, flooding ditches, traditionally laid hedges woven from hawthorn, woven-willow compost bins, a wormery and even an outdoor fireplace. It was an immediate success.

All of the plants used in the display were edible or useful in some way, and included water mint, red clover, valerian, cob nut, hawthorn, elder, wild strawberries, meadow clary, wild thyme and many more. Even though they were planted in an aesthetically pleasing way, the garden itself looked as natural as a country garden in Stow-on-the-Wold. In fact, it made all the other gardens at Chelsea look a trifle contrived in comparison.

After Chelsea finished in 2008, the garden was packed up and moved, plant by plant, to the Daylesford Organic farm in the Cotswolds where it was reconstructed (directly in front of a real wheat field) and used for educational lectures on sustainable living and natural gardening principles. The garden is still in place today, and looks even more spectacular that it did in London.

The centerpiece of the garden is the 'garden kitchen', a green-roofed cottage built using reclaimed timber, Cotswold stone and solar panels. In essence, it's an indoor/outdoor entertaining space but it's so sleek that it thoroughly deserves centre stage. Surrounding this is the kitchen garden itself, which forms a wedge between the building and the wheat field. Here, in woven willow beds, are rows of fruits and vegetables including broad beans, cabbages, lettuces and strawberries. There is also a wormery on one side of the garden, and a collection of pretty bee hives in a wildflower field on the other.

According to Carole Bamford, the garden is a 'living illustration of [Daylesford Organic's] philosophy that farming, and growing plants, leads to a richer, more fulfilling life.'

Cultivation of the soil, she says, puts us in touch with nature. And it is through nature, she adds, that we achieve a sense of spiritual connection.

'A gardener who grows what he eats has a feeling of belonging, which is precious and irreplaceable. Being in harmony with the seasons, and respecting the soil itself, brings meaning to our modern world.'

Daylesford Organic has several stores located throughout London at Notting Hill, Pimlico Road and in Selfridges, but the best place to see the philosophy of the company in action is at the Farmshop at Daylesford, near Kingham in Gloucestershire. The Farmshop comprises a café/restaurant, store, garden, and grocer/butcher in a setting reminiscent of a Cotswold village. The kitchen garden is open to the public by prior arrangement and through the gardening courses. For enquiries, visit www.daylesfordorganic.com, or email enquiries@daylesfordorganic.com

NURTURING THE SOIL FOR FUTURE GENERATIONS

ROTATION AND COMPANION PLANTING

Rotating your vegetables and companion planting utilise the natural properties of some plants to enhance the productivity of others. Three simple planting tips are:

1   Use borage to deter many pests and attract useful insects
2   Plant nasturtiums to manage aphids, pumpkin beetles, squash beetles, cabbage moths, potato beetles and whiteflies
3   Plant chamomile to accumulate useful trace elements, improve the flavour of vegetables and improve the crop size of onions.

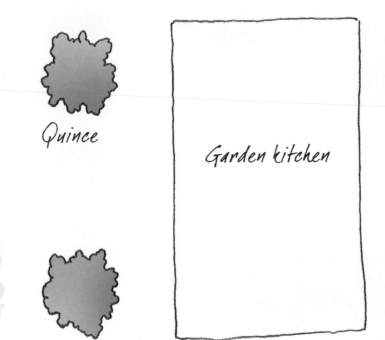

Quince

Garden kitchen

Quince

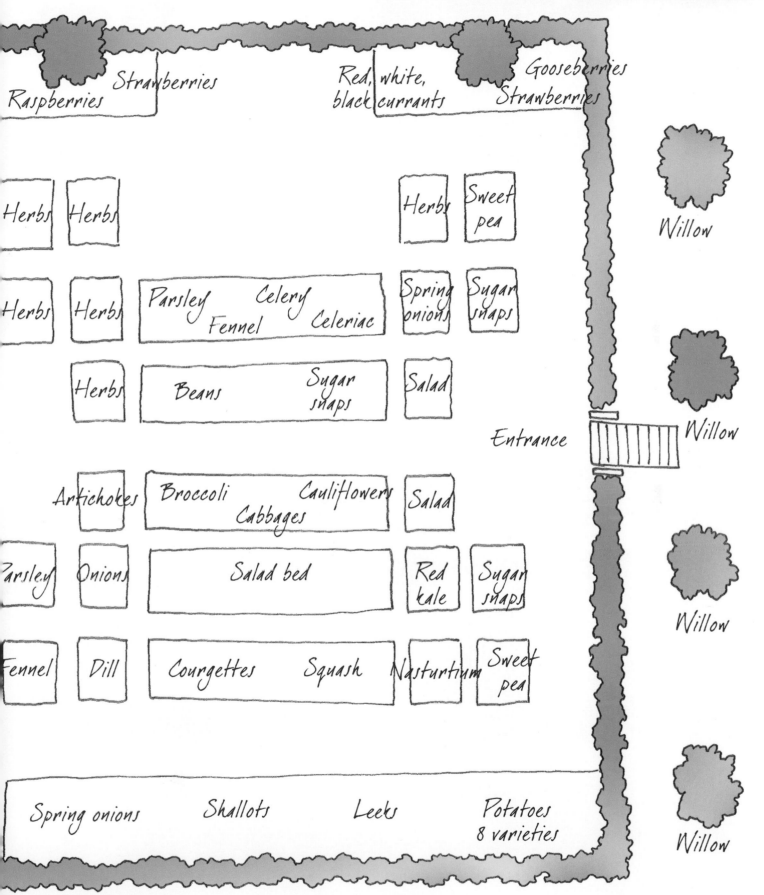

Raspberries

Strawberries

Red, white, black currants

Gooseberries
Strawberries

Herbs   Herbs

Herbs   Sweet pea

Herbs   Herbs

Parsley   Celery
Fennel   Celeriac

Spring onions

Sugar snaps

Herbs

Beans   Sugar snaps

Salad

Willow

Entrance

Willow

Artichokes

Broccoli   Cauliflowers
Cabbages

Salad

Parsley   Onions

Salad bed

Red kale

Sugar snaps

Willow

Fennel   Dill

Courgettes   Squash

Nasturtium

Sweet pea

Spring onions   Shallots   Leeks   Potatoes 8 varieties

Willow

BARNSLEY HOUSE

Should it not be remembered that in setting a garden we are painting a picture?

BEATRIX JONES FARRAND

THE PLANTSWOMAN'S GARDEN

I was fortunate enough to meet Rosemary Verey before she passed away. It was at London's Chelsea Flower Show in the mid-1990s, and it was on Media Day, the day when members of the press are permitted special access to write about the show before the public follows through. There were very few people around on this day, and as I stopped before the Highgrove exhibition, which was an extraordinary replica of His Royal Highness The Prince of Wales' garden in Gloucestershire, I realised that a small, elderly woman had appeared quietly beside me. Thinking it was someone associated with the show, or even a columnist from a country gardening magazine, I smiled and told her that if she wished to know more about the Highgrove display, there would probably be information available at the Media Tent across the way.

'Oh, that's quite alright,' she said. 'I know all about it. I actually helped designed the garden – this one and the real thing at Highgrove. I just wondered what you thought of it. That's all.'

And then, before I could answer – or even apologise profusely for my unintended rudeness – the lovely lady wandered off, ending the conversation.

I was mortified, of course. An opportunity to meet one of the garden world's great names only comes along once in a lifetime, and to miss it through idiocy and ignorance is utterly foolish. I never forgot the encounter, and I never forgave myself for it.

A decade later, I found myself remembering the incident as I pulled into the driveway of Verey's former home, Barnsley House, one summer's afternoon as the golden Cotswold light tipped the treetops and the pink peonies swayed in the breeze.

Both Rosemary Verey and Barnsley House are revered in the horticultural world. Indeed, it is difficult to figure out which is more respected: the writer, or the garden she created. Verey is still considered the *grande dame* of English gardening writers a decade after she passed away, and to prove it, Barnsley House is inundated with visitors season after season, year after year.

Located in the tiny, highly photogenic village of Barnsley, near Cirencester in Gloucestershire, the historic 17th-century rectory came into Verey's life when her husband David Verey inherited the estate in 1951. Until then, she hadn't taken a great deal of interest in gardens or design, but when they settled into their Gloucestershire home, she dedicated herself to the subject matter with tenacity and passion. Her husband, who was an architecture historian, encouraged her in her new pursuit and the estate flourished as a result. Entirely self-taught, she followed her instincts and embraced her mistakes as much as her successes. A garden is an organic experiment, and Verey treated hers as an ongoing education from Mother Nature.

The entire garden at Barnsley House consists of about four acres, but perhaps the most intriguing corner – certainly one of the most written about parts of the garden – is the decorative kitchen garden. It was this garden that earned Verey the title 'Queen of the Potager'. Verey loved the idea of an edible landscape or ornamental vegetable garden – she believed gardens should be both productive and pretty – and spent much of her time there. She also did much to encourage others to follow suit, emboldening other gardeners to bring their kitchen gardens out from behind the shed and into the landscape.

One of the inspirations for the garden was Villandry, the great château potager in France, but Verey's kitchen garden is – as she intended it to be – far more intimate. She wanted it to be on a scale that all gardeners could relate to. (And indeed, such is the charm and design of the potager that it's easy to feel that it would be entirely possible to achieve such a space in one's own garden.)

One of Verey's great gardening strengths was that she had an artist's eye, especially for colour, lines and texture, and because of this, her gardens took on an almost Impressionist quality. Her kitchen garden was no exception. Beds of cabbages were – and still are – colour-coordinated into harmonious shades, from soft

greens to pale pinks, and then interplanted with flowers such as sweet peas to achieve a profusion of tint and scent. (Verey was so fond of sweet peas that one variety is now named after her.) Elsewhere, mauve lavender stalks brush borders with pale green lettuce leaves, and ripe strawberries share soil with pink peonies.

The patterned plantings continue through the potager in such a highly decorative fashion that to wander the paths, even today, is to encounter an extraordinary mix of hues, heights, tints, textures, scents and lines of sight. It is truly gardening as art.

Verey's idea for the underlying design of the kitchen garden was that it should be arranged into four paths that radiated out like a cross. The garden isn't large – perhaps 75 square feet – but its cross-axes give it the feeling of being much grander. (And the four quarters are ideally suited to crop rotation.) Planting in small beds also allows for new plant combinations each year, while the walled enclosure gives it a secluded feel, and keeps the wind out and the heat in. To achieve height, Verey used climbing vegetables and fruit trees, which she trained in whimsical ways.

It was never meant to be a 'grand' garden. Her inspiration was always the 17th-century horticulturist William Lawson, who thought that a kitchen garden should have 'comely borders' with herbs and 'an abundance of roses and lavender', which 'yield much profit, and comfort to the senses'. (She modelled her kitchen garden on a design in William Lawson's book, *A Country Housewife's Garden*, published in 1618).

It was designed to be a garden that could be tended by one person, but that was also capable of feeding an entire family. In short, it was a clever redesign of the classic Victorian kitchen garden: compact, beautiful and useful.

Rosemary Verey wrote about her garden in various books and also gave dozens of talks about it over the years, mostly in America, where she was greatly admired. She was a prolific writer and speaker, and her many books and lectures had an enormous influence on others. It wasn't long before the reputation of her kitchen garden spread worldwide, and visitors from as far as Japan began making the trek to Gloucestershire to see just how the venerable Ms Verey treated her vegetables. There are those, gardening writers among them, who firmly believe that this lovely, unassuming and utterly charming old lady was not only one of the most influential gardeners in the world, but that she was single-handedly responsible for the modern revival of the kitchen garden. After visiting her glorious Gloucestershire garden, I am one of them. I just wish I had told her.

The gardens of Barnsley House at Barnsley, near Cirencester, Gloucestershire, are only open to guests of the hotel (the estate was turned into a hotel after Ms Verey passed away), but it is well worth staying here if you love gardens. If you just want to visit for the day, however, it may be possible to do that. Otherwise, there are several open days each year for the public through the National Gardens Scheme. For details visit www.barnsleyhouse.com

CREATE INTERESTING VISTAS

Rosemary Verey was a genius at creating lines of sight, or vistas, through a garden. You can stand almost anywhere at Barnsley House and be rewarded with a perfect view. Even the potager has views of both the house and the fields beyond. Before you start planning your garden, take a moment to consider any views. Is there any way you can enhance these vistas with the use of paths, gates or planting schemes? Take particular note of where the sun goes down, as gardeners are often out in the late afternoon, gathering plants for dinner or simply pottering around. Try to position a seat so it faces the sunset: it will make a wonderful place to end the day. Make the views a priority, and your garden will be full of theatre and drama.

ROOM 10
"THE POTTING SHED"

USING GARDEN ARCHITECTURE TO GROW UP RATHER THAN OUT

Many gardeners are now thinking like architects and using all of the available space, not just the land available on the ground. Rosemary Verey, for example, trained gooseberries, red currants and raspberries to grow against walls and fences, and espaliered the branches of fruit trees so they stretched out sideways. She also introduced the 'pea tunnel', which was a rose arch covered in peas, offering visitors a delightful entrance to the kitchen garden while providing space beneath for other plants. At other times the pea tunnel also featured zucchini with yellow blossoms and beans with red flowers. Verey also planted the spare patches between plants with peonies, lavender, roses and herbs, so the air always smelled lovely. Other gardeners are using architecture to enhance their kitchen gardens by building 'gourd tunnels', or weaving wattling wigwams and other sculptural frames to grow zucchini, beans, peas and tomatoes on.

THINK OF YOUR GARDEN AS A PAINTING

All gardens – even kitchen gardens – need to be considered as living art. As Beatrix Jones Farrand once said: 'Should it not be remembered that in setting a garden we are painting a picture?' Thinking of your garden as art also makes it easier to decide on colour schemes. What kind of paintings or art do you prefer? If you love Monet's Giverny series, plant purple and white irises, snow peas and other mauve, pink and yellow flowers and vegetables. You could even design a miniature water lily pond with a bridge. If you prefer bold, bright art, plant big, bright, attention-grabbing flowers and vegetables. Or if you like edgy, modern sculpture, consider installing some in your garden. One woman who loved purple planted a garden that was full of it – aubergines, beans, grapes and even purple carrots. It sounds crazy, but she enjoyed being in her garden that much more because it was full of her favourite colour.

Rose hedge

Carrots
Lettuce

Cauliflower
Leeks

Trained apples

Seed bed

Broad beans

Strawberries

Onions

Strawberries

Lettuce
Red
cabbage

Lettuce/French beans

N

Mint

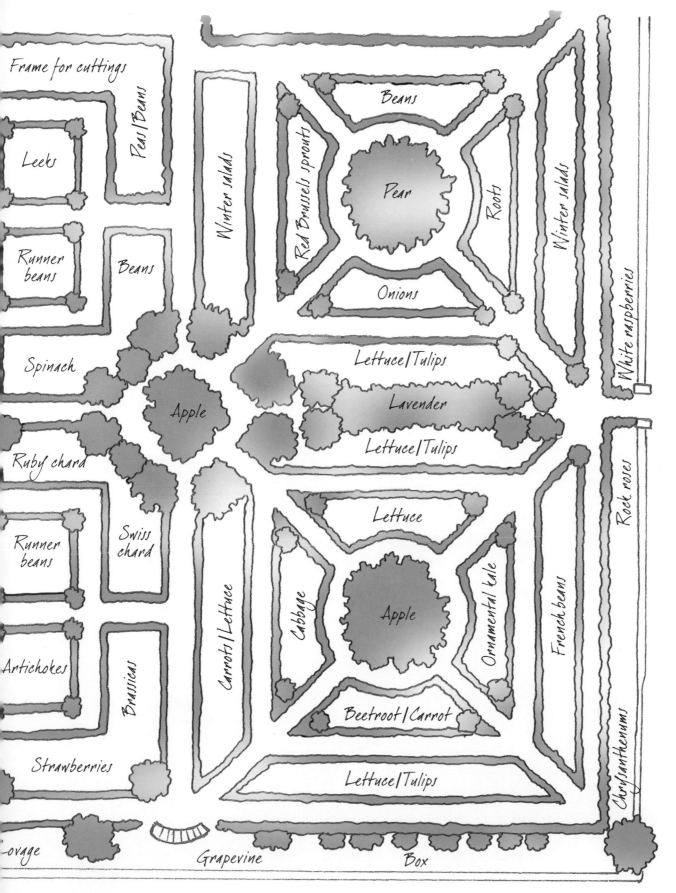

Frame for cuttings

Peas/Beans

Leeks

Runner beans

Beans

Spinach

Ruby chard

Swiss chard

Runner beans

Artichokes

Brassicas

Strawberries

Lovage

Apple

Winter salads

Carrots/Lettuce

Grapevine

Beans

Red Brussels sprouts

Pear

Onions

Lettuce/Tulips

Lavender

Lettuce/Tulips

Lettuce

Cabbage

Apple

Ornamental kale

Beetroot/Carrot

Lettuce/Tulips

Box

French beans

Roots

Winter salads

White raspberries

Rock roses

Chrysanthemums

PRIEURÉ DE NOTRE-DAME D'ORSAN

The best place to find God is in a garden.
You can dig for him there.
GEORGE BERNARD SHAW

THE PRIORY GARDEN

Of all the gardens in the world, there are a handful that come up in conversation, blogs, mainstream media and magazines year after year. These are the gardens that stand out from the horticultural crowd, the gardens that offer such distinction that they become destinations in their own right. Every gardener should see them at least once in their life, if possible. The potager at Villandry is one of them. The Prieuré de Notre-Dame d'Orsan is another.

Tucked away in Berry, near the Loire Valley, the Prieuré de Notre-Dame d'Orsan is so hidden that it is quite difficult to find – but keep trying, because it is worth the meandering drive through the French countryside. This remarkable 60-acre garden is unlike anything in the world. It is gardening at its most magical.

Designed by Parisian architect Patrice Taravella and his former partner, designer Sonia Lesot, the garden is set on the ruins of a medieval cloister that dates from the 12th century. The garden is based on gardens of pre-Renaissance times, so consequently everything here is monastically simple and delightfully restrained, providing an unexpected sense of serenity.

Seats, arches and trellises are all made from long, slender twigs woven into place. Raised vegetable beds are fashioned out of a similar kind of basketwork, while hedges form buttressed arches over paths. Even the rhubarb is grown in beautiful natural 'tubs' made from woven vine. Elsewhere, plants, bushes and fruit trees are pruned with painstaking care into enchanting shapes.

It is a garden designed to evoke the spirit – and spirituality – of a medieval garden, and it does so with grace and elegance.

Indeed, it is so peaceful that walking through it is like undertaking a walking meditation.

'The dream was to recreate the spirit of the medieval priory,' explains Patrice Taravella, who bought the garden in 1991 when it was almost derelict. Using function, symbolism and aesthetics as their three key guidelines, the couple meticulously researched the designs of medieval gardens, including the way they were divided and the ways in which frames, raised beds, hedges and other structures were created and used. It was a case of employing function *and* form, rather than form over function or vice versa.

However, there is also a fourth element that has been integrated into this design – humour. The garden is full of cheeky and light-hearted touches, from ivy that's been shaped into hearts to charming peepholes that have been carved out of hedges to offer lovely lines of sight through the garden rooms beyond.

As was the case with medieval gardens that were tended by monks, the majority of plants grown in this garden are for consumption, and the ways in which the gardeners integrate fruit and vegetables into the design is pure genius. Instead of filling the parterres with flowers, for example, the gardeners often plant wheat, broad beans, leeks or cabbages. The Maze Vegetable Garden, meanwhile, is a labyrinth made of pleached plums and gages interspersed with beds of herbs and vegetables, while the Berry Path, an enchanting long walk, is festooned with myriad varieties of berries on either side, including raspberries trained on V-shaped poles for ease of picking. There are more than 20 varieties of apples grown in the orchard, including *Querine*

Florina, Patte de loup and *Drap d'or,* and there are also delightful walls of espaliered pears dressing the main entrance building.

The garden was the winner of the *Institut de France* garden prize, and the head gardener, Gilles Guillot, has been elected best gardener in France by the *Demeure Historique*. The property was also awarded the title of 'Remarkable Garden' by the Ministry of Culture. Walking through this place, it is easy to see why France loves it so much.

The Prieuré de Notre-Dame d'Orsan (Priory of Our Lady of Orsan) is located at Maisonnais in Berry, France, and is open to the public. See www.prieuredorsan.com or email prieuredorsan@wanadoo.fr for further details about the garden and hotel.

USING NATURAL MATERIALS TO CREATE GARDEN ARCHITECTURE

The remarkable garden at Prieuré d'Orsan is famous for many things, but the element that has really captured the attention – and imagination – of visitors is the way natural materials have been used to create spectacular garden architecture. In line with the garden's philosophy and historic origins, these natural materials create a back-to-basics beauty that sits harmoniously with the garden's gentle aesthetic and monastic feel. The architecture created by these natural materials has been so effective at Prieuré d'Orsan that countless visitors have returned home to their own gardens and tried to emulate the elegant simplicity with pruned branches, willows and vines – and Prieuré proves that it's not difficult to do. Natural materials such as willow, vines, bamboo or pruned branches are inexpensive, because they're often readily available on properties, and they are environmentally friendly and easy to construct. The thing to remember is to match the material to the structure. For example, if you're creating a rustic obelisk, look for strong, sturdy, straight branches so they won't blow away in the wind and will withstand climbers. Be sure to brace obelisks by ensuring that a significant portion of the legs are buried in the ground. A pyramidal trellis, which is one of the easiest structures to make, can be used in a potager to help beans and other climbers, while a simple, two-dimensional trellis can be used to create windbreaks and screening.

N

MONTSALVAT

Gardens are the result of a collaboration between art and nature.
PENELOPE HOBHOUSE

Wandering through Montsalvat is like wandering through a romantic ruin that has been brought back to life. In fact, Montsalvat isn't really a ruin (since it's been impressively restored over the years) but more a wondrous, completely overwhelming ode to lost architecture. It's rustic, yes, but glamorously, gorgeously so. Rustic seems too coarse a word for it. It's simply marvellous.

Montsalvat resembles a small French village, only an extremely atmospheric, beautifully designed one, as if Hollywood had had a say in the planning. It was the idea of artist Justus Jörgensen, who started building it in 1934. Previously a student of the well-known artist Max Meldrum, Jörgensen had spent a great deal of time painting at Eltham – which was, at the time, a rural region north of Melbourne that was beloved by artists – and knew the area well. He wanted to create an artists' colony here, much like Heide further west, and set about designing a 'village' on 12 acres of bushland. It was intended to be a unique complex of buildings made largely from earth, stone and recycled materials. Because it was built by Jörgensen and his students and friends, rather than proper builders, and constructed of mostly recycled materials, it took longer than normal to complete. In fact, construction continued for years.

Jörgensen wasn't too perturbed by this. He saw the organic process as being part of the personality of Montsalvat, and a way of teaching his students practical skills and patience.

Eventually the village took shape, albeit in a range of rustic architectural styles, with a chapel, a dairy, stables, storehouses, residences and even a Great Hall.

Soon the reputation of Montsalvat as a place of creativity and inspiration spread. Artists came from far and wide to see the magnificent place. They came, and they stayed, which was Jörgensen's intention all along.

More than 70 years on, they're still coming, and still taking up residence in the various cottages. Only now, they're joined by thousands of visitors who flock here to wander the village paths, gaze in wonder at the historic architecture, shake their heads at the beauty of the landscape and grounds and wish that they, too, could have a Montsalvat cottage to call their own.

Most of these visitors congregate around the Great Hall and the pool, but there is another corner of the property that is just as charming, and that's the kitchen garden. Tucked away behind a wonderfully whimsical chicken coop and a collection of gorgeous glasshouses, the garden is managed by volunteers. It's more of a rambling jumble of plants than a carefully designed potager, but the gentle mess of it only adds to its character. Fruit and vegetables grown in this delightfully relaxed garden are used in the Monsalvat restaurant, The Meeting Pool. The glasshouses and conservatories alongside the garden are really worth seeing – they look like something from Victorian England. Some of them are used as studios (one has a fashion designer working out of it and is therefore filled with fabrics and mannequins), while others are left to pots and plants. Even the rusty garden gates and the ivy that twines itself around the buildings seem to sit in architectural harmony with the rest of the garden.

Montsalvat is open seven days a week. For details, visit www.montsalvat.com.au

Photograph courtesy Monsalvat

GREENHOUSE GRANDEUR

The beauty of Montsalvat is in its architecture, and particularly its greenhouses, potting sheds and other intriguing outbuildings. Some of these outbuildings may be a little past their heyday, but their faded grandeur only makes them that much more endearing. They also show that a garden can be greatly enhanced by the addition of a charming outbuilding, whether it's a greenhouse, a small conservatory, a potting shed or even a cute chook shed. And of course, these buildings don't have to be used for their original purpose! Many artists, writers and designers, such as those who work at Montsalvat, love working in old buildings because they inspire and delight in equal measure.

THE ROOFTOP GARDEN

NEW YORK

Plants give us oxygen for the lungs and for the soul.

LINDA SOLEGATO

New York's East Village is an intriguing, bohemian place known for its creativity and artistic sensibility. In recent years, it has also become known for its gardens. No one can work out whether this is an extension of the East Village's long-held interest in aesthetics, or a reaction against the increasing cacophony and urban stress of city living. Whatever the reason, gardens are growing here – and they're growing extraordinary well. It's as if all the East Village's residents have suddenly discovered they've got green thumbs.

Featured in the patchwork of green spaces in the 'Verdant Village' (as some people are now calling it) are community gardens, private gardens, tiny gardens, luxuriant gardens, humble gardens, lush sanctuaries of calm and crowded, raucous areas where canines and humans play happily together. There are tiny plots squeezed between buildings, balconies overflowing with plants, 'casita' gardens with Latin-flavoured landscaping, English cottage-style spaces, arty gardens with sculptures and of course the tree-lined streets themselves, which are part of the fabulously eclectic East Village landscape. Then there are rooftop gardens. It's these gardens that are really causing the East Village's residents to look up and take notice.

Someone who knows all about the East Village's rooftop gardens is Paula Crossfield, who was so inspired by the green activity around her that she devised a plan to design a garden of her very own.

The name behind the popular food and gardening blog Civil Eats (Civileats.com), Paula noticed that New Yorkers were taking more of an interest in where they spent their leisure time (in the city's gardens) and where the food they ate came from. What better way to combine the two than to design a rooftop garden? A rooftop garden, she reasoned, would offer a place to retreat to from the madness of Manhattan while providing fresh, homegrown produce for those who lived below. It was also the perfect way to utilise a valuable part of the building that had been left languishing, as well as making the most of the building's spectacular views.

The first step was to refurbish the 1000-square-foot roof of the six-floor walk-up, which, to their credit, her Lower East Side co-op organised. The second step was to persuade fellow board members to spend $3000 to create a 400-square-foot garden on it by building planters and paving part of the roof. They did that, too.

Paula, who lives on the top floor with her husband, agreed to not only pay for the seeds and do all the harvesting, but also to share the bounty with her neighbours. She didn't realise the idea would be such a success. Nearly a year later, the rooftop garden is flourishing and the residents are not only reaping the rewards of the lush vegetable beds, they are also using the outdoor space as a place to chill out, no matter what the season.

Some of the vegetables that have been harvested include tomatoes, cucumbers, oakleaf lettuce, rainbow chard, Brussels sprouts, butternut squash, zucchini and even watermelon. High above the noise and grime of the urban streets, the garden is thriving. And the views? Well, some residents believe that the sight of a fresh lettuce beats even the vista of the Empire State Building that the rooftop offers.

FINDING THE SPACE FOR A GARDEN

This New York rooftop garden shows that you can plant a potager anywhere, even in the smallest spaces. If you only have a small area to create a kitchen garden, be it a terrace, balcony, verandah or beside the kitchen door, it is possible to grow your favourite produce. All you need is somewhere that receives four to six hours of sunlight a day, either directly or reflected off a wall, and a planting area with at least 30 centimetres of soil. Pots are great but so are planter boxes. (If you're planting bigger plants, such as eggplants, tomatoes, cucumbers, and so on, you'll need a big pot, something bigger than 20 litres.) If you're doubtful about how much space you have, companies such as the Diggers Club supply mini-varieties of vegetables like carrots and cauliflowers. Try to grow what you love, as you'll be more inclined to look after and nourish the garden when you love eating what's in it. And don't forget, you can always grow up – varieties such as beans, peas, pumpkins, apples and pears can easily be trained to grow up a trellis, saving space on your balcony, verandah or terrace for you to sit back and relax with a drink.

LAST WORDS

Your first job is to prepare the soil. The best tool for this is your neighbor's garden tiller.

If your neighbor does not own a garden tiller, suggest that he buy one.

DAVE BARRY

I don't like broccoli. And I haven't liked it since I was a little kid and my mother made me eat it. And I'm President of the United States and I'm not going to eat any more broccoli.

GEORGE H. W. BUSH, FORMER US PRESIDENT

INDEX

ACKNOWLEDGEMENTS

The Images Publishing Group and Janelle McCulloch would like to sincerely thank the following owners of the public and private gardens for their kind contribution to this book.

Stephenie Alexander from the Stephanie Alexander Kitchen Garden Foundation; Sir Anthony Bamford, Lady Bamford and Camilla Wilson from Daylesford Organic; Gael and Francesco Boglione and Charlotte Senn from Petersham House; Henvi Carvallo from Château de Villandry; Château de Rivau; Paula Crossfield; Neil and Angela Davey from the London allotment; the Ecole National Superieure du Paysage, which manages Le Potager du Roi; Jonathan Goh from the Royal Botanic Gardens Melbourne; John van Haandel and former head chef Matt Wilkinson from Circa at The Prince; Max Jörgensen, Sigmund Jörgensen and Claire Crawford from Montsalvat; Karen Keal and Charlotte Doherty from Barnsley House; Paul and Gabrielle Preat from Larundel; Mickey and Larry Robertston from Glenmore House; Patrice Taravella and Sonia Lesot from Prieuré d'Orsan; Ruth Williams and Scott Carlin from Vaucluse House.

Image of Spray Farm, Victoria, on page 20, by Janelle McCulloch.

Other titles from The Images Publishing Group

Coast: Lifestyle Architecture

Janelle McCulloch

ISBN: 978 1 86470 331 3

Seaside architecture is often stunning in its simplicity and grace, its integration of form and function. *Coast: Lifestyle Architecture* offers readers a rare insight into a selection of truly extraordinary seaside homes.

Ranging from sea captains' mansions to smaller-scale architectural treasures, *Coast* presents a collection of beach houses built by renowned designers. All the homes presented in this beautiful book are distinctive and individual, but all share an intimate relationship with their setting — coastal homes, perhaps more than any other, embrace their natural environment, with inside flowing effortlessly into outside.

Coast is a delightful journey into a world of sensitive architecture, sand and sea — it is a must-have for architects, designers and anyone who is drawn to the relaxed and rhythmic pace of seaside life.

Paris Secrets: Architecture, Interiors, Quartiers, Corners

Janelle McCulloch

ISBN: 978 1 86470 308 5

Mixing aesthetics, architecture, arrondissements and elegance in a very Parisian way, *Paris Secrets: Architecture, Interiors, Quartiers, Corners* shows the world's most bewitching city in all its light, shade, glamour and grandeur.

From magnificent squares to exquisite side streets, tucked-away gardens to quiet neighbourhood bistros, and of course the architecture, interiors and style for which Paris is so famous, this richly illustrated volume shows the sophistication and grace that underline the City of Light. Wind your way through Paris via pages shimmering with seductive stairwells, irresistible bistros and patisseries, beguiling back streets, beautiful boulevards, enticing courtyards and must-see interiors.

A modern guide for the urban aesthete, this gorgeous book is both an insightful travel resource and an architectural study that captures Paris's elegance and atmosphere in spectacular detail.

Cloudehill: A Year in the Garden

Jeremy Francis

ISBN: 978 1 86470 377 1

Cloudehill: A Year in the Garden tells the story of Cloudehill nursery, one of Australia's finest gardens and nurseries, and a world-class destination. Located at the top of Melbourne's Dandenong ranges, Cloudehill was originally inspired by the famous Arts & Crafts gardens of England and today features an extraordinary collection of rare and sought-after plants.

Cloudehill's owner-turned-author Jeremy Francis presents the story of Cloudehill, intertwined with an engaging family history beginning with his childhood on a remote farm in Western Australia, his subsequent farming career, and his eventual guardianship of Cloudehill. Intimate diary entries paralleling the gardening year are interspersed, granting an unforgettable insight into the author's passionate relationship with the land. This spectacular book is beautifully illustrated with detailed photographs.

Garden Details: Ideas. Inspiration. Great Garden Spaces

Marg Thornell and Kate Thornell

ISBN: 978 1 86470 234 7

A garden, whether small or large, is made up of many different elements and details. Grouping these design elements is like a recipe; choosing a balance of the right details creates a perfect garden in any space.

Garden Details: Ideas. Inspiration. Great Garden Spaces is a valuable sourcebook that breaks down garden elements and shows how each can be used to create unique garden spaces. It includes ideas for a multitude of garden elements – from distinctive stonewalls and manicured formal lines to artistic whimsy and colour coordinated borders – in a variety of garden types ranging from water gardens through to drought-tolerant dry gardens.

Through hundreds of sumptuous photographs featuring gardens in locations as diverse as Australia, England, Europe and the United States, *Garden Details* reveals how to use detail to make the most of your own garden space.

The information and illustrations in this publication have been prepared and supplied
by Janelle McCulloch. While all reasonable efforts have been made to ensure
accuracy, the publishers do not, under any circumstances, accept responsibility
for errors, omissions and representations express or implied.